PRAISE FOR SOMEWHERE I BELONG

Compelling from its first sentence to its last, *Somewhere I Belong* tells the story of a young woman's hard-won coming-of-age in the waning days of apartheid South Africa and beyond. From her Eastern-European Jewish ancestors' arrival in rural South Africa to her parents' fierce efforts to assimilate and prosper, Berelowitz traces a complex familial and cultural history, creating a vivid tapestry of a volatile time. It's thrilling—and sometimes harrowing—to watch this brilliant and passionate young woman make her way through a treacherous era full of false promises and subtle traps and somehow prevail. The author would ultimately become an art historian and university professor, and her keen eye for the concealed detail, the disputed date, the way "small flashes of illumination" [cast] light onto shadow" make for wonderful reading. Lyrical and full of suspense, this memoir is a gem of observation, imagination, and courage.

—**Marjorie Sandor,** author of *The Secret Music at Tordesillas*

As an art historian reading the work of a fellow scholar, I was enchanted by Jo-Anne Berelowitz' beautifully crafted autofiction of her life, first in apartheid-era South Africa and later as an immigrant in California. With the sophistication of Jane Austen in revealing character and mores through description of lived spaces, Berelowitz' gripping narrative is enriched by analyses of personally meaningful artworks and collections. This wonderful book will particularly resonate with anyone who has explored their own identity and heritage.

—**Allyson Burgess Williams, Ph.D.** Author of "Rewriting Lucrezia Borgia: Propriety, Magnificence, and Piety in Portraits of a Renaissance Duchess." In *Wives, Widows, Mistresses, and Nuns in Early Modern Italy*

Probing, richly layered, and beautifully written, *Somewhere I Belong* is a masterful blend of the remembered and the imagined. The author's personal story, mostly set in apartheid South Africa, is gripping. "Don't think of this place as home," Berelowitz's father tells his ten-year-old daughter, who has never lived anywhere else. Thus begins a lifelong quest for belonging which, while the author's own, poses questions pertinent to us all.

—**Nancy Geyer,** Pushcart prize-winning essayist, recipient of the 2025 Terry Tempest Williams Prize in Creative Nonfiction

With eloquent intimacy, this memoir artfully navigates childhood, university life, marriage, and emigration from apartheid South Africa. The journey continues in California with motherhood and marital dissolution, but with subsequent academic achievement, triumphant self-assertion, and love. Dislocations and crises may delay the author's sense of belonging, but her book belongs in your hands and on your bookshelf.

—**David Reifler,** *Days of Ticho: Empire, Mandate, Medicine and Art in the Holy Land*

Joanne Berelowitz is a master of lyric prose. *In Somewhere I Belong*, she weaves personal accounts, historical facts, and acquired insights into a moving and memorable story. Demonstrating keen intellectual and emotional curiosity, coupled with steadfast determination as a lifelong learner, she engages the reader in her exploration of Jewish heritage, the apartheid South African culture in which she was reared, and, ultimately, in finding the place where she belongs.

Lori Kline, author of *Almost a Minyan* and *Josiah's Dreams*

Jo-Anne Berelowitz is a gifted writer and art historian. *In Somewhere I Belong*, she weaves a stunning tapestry of history, country, and the complexities of relationships. She brilliantly lures readers into her unique story—from her generational roots to being on the receiving end of the ultimate family betrayal.

—**Monique Faison Ross,** author of *Playing Dead: A Memoir of Terror and Survival*

Jo-Anne Berelowitz's book, *Somewhere I Belong*, describes her search to understand her family's journeys of survival and navigation of Jewish identity. From the pogroms of Lithuania to apartheid South Africa, then outward again to the U.S. and England, Berelowitz explores how place, time and zeitgeist pressure, mold, and re-mold Jewish identity. Even as she doggedly pursues knowledge and understanding, she accepts the white spaces created by lack of source material, treating those spaces with the deft imagination of an ancient Midrashist. Beautifully written, with love and compassion for both her forebears and her own questions of identity, this book is a gift to all Diaspora Jews seeking to understand the eternal questions of how and why Jewish identity expresses itself in relation to the pressing present moment, wherever we find ourselves.

—**Cathy Schechter**, author of *Deep in the Heart: The Lives and Legends of Texas Jews* (with Ruthe Winegarten)

Somewhere I Belong

A STORY OF
COUNTRY, FAMILY, HOME,
AND JEWISH IDENTITY

JO-ANNE BERELOWITZ

DIASPORA
PRESS

Copyright © 2025 by Jo-Anne Berelowitz

All rights reserved. No part of this book may be used or reproduced in any manner whatsoever without written permission except in the case of brief quotations embodied in critical articles or reviews.

Published by Diaspora Press

DIASPORA
PRESS

Printed in the United States of America
10 9 8 7 6 5 4 3 2 1

Produced by GMK Writing and Editing, Inc.
Managing Editor: Katie Benoit
Copyedited by Kelly Clody
Proofread by: Elizabeth Crooks
Text design and composition by Libby Kingsbury
Cover design by Libby Kingsbury
Printed by IngramSpark

Print ISBN: 978-1-966981-04-6
Ebook ISBN: 978-1-966981-05-3

Visit the author at www.joanneberelowitz.com

Three chapters were previously published in literary journals:

"Portrait #1: Paternal Grandfather Joseph: A Memoir in Midrashim" was published in the *Colorado Review*, 50.2, Summer 2023 as "Looking for Joseph: A Memoir in Midrashim."

"Epiphany" was published in the *Sycamore Review*, 30th Anniversary Issue, Vol. 30, Issue 1, Summer/Fall 2018, under the same title and was awarded the 2018 Wabash Prize for Nonfiction.

A shorter version of "Empty Bookshelves" was published in *The Hong Kong Review, An International Journal of Literature, Culture, and the Arts*, January 2020, Vol. 2, No. 1 as "Tears."

Note to the reader:

These are my memories; the conversations are not verbatim transcripts; they are as I recall them and, as such, are my truth. Actors in my story may, if asked, recall things differently and have different versions of what I recount—even of the same incidents. They have as much right to their stories, their truth, as I do to mine.

The starting point is my father, Morris Abraham Berelowitz (1919–2019) z"l, to whom this book is dedicated. May his memory be a blessing.

> . . . *you cannot move on without the memory of where you come from, even if that journey is fictitious.*
> —BREYTEN BREYTENBACH, *Dog Year*

> . . . *all art is deception.*
> —VLADIMIR NABOKOV, *Strong Opinions*

> *The name on the title page is not the proper name of a subject capable of self-knowledge and understanding. . . . Autobiography veils a defacement of the mind of which it is itself the cause.*
> —PAUL DE MAN, "Autobiography as Defacement," The Rhetoric of Romanticism

Acknowledgments

Many people helped me on my journey to complete this book, and I am deeply grateful. Their love and support have been gifts beyond rubies.

My first thanks are to my husband, who has always believed in me—even when I didn't. His steadfast love kept me going.

There are many others: my family; my writing mentor and friend, Marjorie Sandor; Rich Farrell and the writing group at San Diego's Writer's Ink; Eustacia Riley; Gray Buccigross; GMK Writing and Editing, Inc.; Stephanie G'Schwind, editor of the *Colorado Review* who unhesitatingly published my personal essay, "Looking for Joseph: A Memoir in Midrashim," when so many journals were blacklisting Jewish writers; the Jewish Book Council; my Mussar vad: our teacher extraordinaire, Cathy Schechter, and fellow students David Wharton, Harriett Kirsh Pozen, Monique Faison Ross, Nancyellen Seiden, and Lisa Greenberg. Last but not least is the embracing Jewish community here in Austin under the inspiring leadership of Rabbi Neil Blumofe and Rabbi Gail Swedroe; I had not realized until I found Agudas Achim how hungry I was for such a community—imbued with the richness of Jewish learning, joy, and chesed.

And then there was Max, beloved fifteen-year-old Soft Coated Wheaten Terrier, constant and beloved canine companion. His fragile presence reminded me every day to be grateful for the gift of life.

Additionally, I am grateful to you, who hold this book in your hands or view it on your screen, for journeying with me. Hopefully, you, too, will find, or have already found, your place of belonging.

Table of Contents

PROLOGUE: January 2020, El Camino Memorial Park, Sorrento Valley, California 1

PART 1: SOUTH AFRICA 3

CHAPTER 1: Fishing in Durban Harbor, 1960 5

CHAPTER 2: Jewish Men Running: Three Portraits 12
   Portrait #1 Paternal Grandfather Joseph: A Memoir in Midrashim 13
   Portrait #2: Maternal Grandfather Sydney: A "Memoranda" 36
   Portrait #3: My Father: Man About Town 59

CHAPTER 3: Reasons to Leave 66
   Cato Manor 66
   A Wind of Change 85

CHAPTER 4: Girlhood to Young Adulthood 90
   Musgrave Road 90
   Not Learning Afrikaans 96
   Mangoes 100
   Love and Letters 107
   Epiphany 113
   Indiscretion 122

CHAPTER 5: Leaving 129

PART 2: NEW WORLD, NEW LIFE 137

CHAPTER 6: California 138
   First Thanksgiving 143
   Empty Bookshelves 156
   Consequences 161

CHAPTER 7: Work, Love, Return 173

CHAPTER 8: Letters and Cards 181
   An Archive 181
   Mother's Day 190

CHAPTER 9: Leaving California, Finding Home 198

EPILOGUE 203

Dreaming of Home

We want so much to be in that place
where we are respected and cherished,
protected, acknowledged,
nurtured, encouraged, heard.

And seen, seen
in all our loveliness,
in all our fragile strength.

And safe, safe in all our trembling
vulnerability. Where we are known
and safe, safe and known--
is it possible?

Merle Feld

Prologue

*January 2020, El Camino Memorial Park
Sorrento Valley, California*

I'm lying on my back atop my father's grave, my bones aligned over his. We buried him yesterday, two weeks after his one hundredth birthday. The only graveside attendees were my mother, my two brothers and their wives, my sister and her husband, my son, my nephews, and my husband.

A rabbi officiated. *Of course*, you might think, but there was no *of course* to the rabbi's presence, for my father had hated all religion, especially his own, though in this, as with almost everything, he was riven by conflict, both rejecting and cleaving to his Jewishness. Despising rabbis and Jewish ritual, he tried to elicit promises from his family that we would not recite the Kaddish on his behalf—that ancient Aramaic prayer affirming life that Jews have recited since the thirteenth century when the Crusaders, en route to the Holy Land, massacred Jews in the Rhineland.

One of my brothers, the one most like my father, gave him the promise he'd sought and turned his back when the rabbi led us in prayer. The rest of us, having made no promise we knew we would not keep, joined the rabbi in chanting. Were we, in defying my father's wishes, disrespectful, or were the imperatives of an ancient practice and the needs of the living reasons enough to override an apostate's wish?

Yit-ga-dal v'yit-ka-dash sh'mei

Ra-ba b'al-ma di-v'ra chir-u-tei

Lying atop my father's bones, I thought about my family and the long journeys we've taken since leaving South Africa so many years ago. I use the plural—journey*s*—because our trajectories and routes have been different. But behind each lay the single driving force of our father, Morris Abraham Berelowitz, who told us we'd have to leave South Africa and find homes elsewhere. And so, because we loved and trusted him, we shook the dust of our natal country off our shoes and embarked on our searches.

I searched for a long while, but now I know where I belong. It's a place my father would have been appalled by. But for me, it's home.

PART 1: SOUTH AFRICA

1

Fishing in Durban Harbor, 1960

MY DAD PRICKS HIS FINGER ON THE HOOK, GODDAMMIT! AND throws the offending shrimp into the bay. He's clumsy threading bait, clumsy with most things. Again, he tries and fails, tries and fails; his finger drips blood, his curses grow louder, and my anxiety mounts. But then, success! He casts our lines, wipes his bloody finger on a rag, and we settle down to wait for grunter to bite.

It's 1960. We're on folding chairs quayside in a gap between berthed cargo ships in Durban Harbor. My brother, Michael, four, is on our dad's left; my sister, Vicki, seven, is on his right; I, ten, am beside her. We're grateful for the afternoon breeze that wafts off the Indian Ocean and cools our damp skin. We're lightly clad—my dad in long khaki shorts; socks that go, South African fashion, up to his knees; and a short-sleeved shirt unbuttoned at the neck. My mother told him to wear a hat, but he doesn't like being told what to do. Defiant, he left it in the car: *Don't tell your mother!* No need to request our complicity; we're already his allies.

His thick hair, flecked with gray, is darker than his gingery mustache, his eyebrows are bushy, and his nose prominent. To me, he seems big, though he's only five-foot-eight, the runt of his parents' litter, a middle child hemmed between much taller brothers, the

My parents on Durban's beachfront, 1960s.

undersized son of parents unusually tall for Litvaks—Lithuanian Jews, 40,000 of whom immigrated to South Africa between 1880 and 1914.

My father, Michael, and Vicki watch the lines for signs of a nibble. I look across the bay and think about its history—the subject of my homework this past week. In 1497 Portuguese explorer Vasco da Gama sheltered his galleons here on Christmas Day. Pious, he named the bay and the land extending beyond *Natal*, Portuguese for *birth of Christ*. In 1835 British settlers founded the city of Durban, naming it for Sir Benjamin D'Urban, a governor of the Cape Colony, a man as brutal to the indigenous Xhosa population as the Cape's first colonial administrator, Jan van Riebeeck, was to the Khoisan whom he enslaved after arriving at the Cape on April 6, 1652. In 1866, when enormous reserves of diamonds were discovered on the south bank of the Orange River, and in 1886, when the world's richest gold deposits were discovered in the rebel Boer Republic of the Transvaal, Durban's harbor and railroad systems became crucial for the flow of goods to and from the interior. Today, it's the largest and busiest shipping terminal in sub-Saharan Africa and the fourth largest container terminal in the Southern Hemisphere.

It's hard to imagine when this region looked like the drawing in my history book, which shows the bay in 1497: sand dunes, riverine, swamps, and mangrove; banana trees, forest honeysuckles, orchids, and cycads; a subtropical paradise where leopards, crocodiles, hippos, monkeys, adders, and mamboes were once wild and at home. Now it has huge container vessels with strange names from distant lands, tugboats guiding big liners to their berths, giant cranes offloading heavy equipment, stevedores shouting in English and Zulu, gulls screeching and swooping for scraps at the whaling station where dead whales are hauled up a slipway to be processed. Sharks, lured by blood, circle the waters.

Squeezing my eyes half shut, I try to place the history book's black-and-white illustration over the scene before me, to see *through* it to the distant past. I can't do it.

But I'm not here to picture the past; I'm not even here for the fishing, which I don't care for. I'm here to be with my dad, to listen to him muse and tell stories of his boyhood in the small Afrikaans-speaking dorp in the Western Cape where his Yiddish-speaking parents, Joseph and Bella, raised him and his two brothers. Michael, Vicki, and I have heard his stories many times, but we never tire of the enigma that our dad was once a boy in a time and place so different from ours. He, gratified by our attention, delights in the retelling: boy scouting in the Outeniqua Mountains and forests of Tsitsikamma, where he once saw the tracks of elephants and, terrified, ran in the opposite direction; attending his father in their small, stuffy dry goods store while Joseph, in his slow, meticulous way, checked and rechecked every line in the accounts book, straining the patience of my bored, fidgety father; his pride in having given the same bar mitzvah speech in English, Yiddish, and Afrikaans—*the* experience, he always adds, that made him love making speeches. After his stories come life lessons, maxims he's gathered over the years and sets great store by: *the unexamined life is not worth living, we must to our own selves be true, life is made of hills and valleys, the strong give in to the weak, follow the golden mean, religion is the opiate of the masses, build bridges between people, be proactive.*

Our dad's a connoisseur of catchy phrases. He rolls them over his tongue the way he drinks Cape wine, attending to their mouthfeel, texture, resonance, and finish. No matter how often he partakes of them, he never exhausts their pleasure but gives each its due, as though struck afresh by its rightness.

As much as we delight in our dad's stories, we find comfort in his philosophizing. When he's on a roll, we don't ask questions. We know he prefers exposition to explanation, that questions interrupt his flow and annoy him, that he gives deep thought to whatever he speaks of and knows his conclusions are right. Like squirrels we store his words for the future, a precious moral code of clichés that will become integral to how we see the world, to how we navigate our small corner of it. His words engrave themselves on our hearts.

This summer day, quayside, he will share words we've not heard before, though we will hear them many times in the years to come. They are words that will drive our future as his mission becomes ours.

A tugboat sounds a long mournful warning. My father, about to speak, pauses for the sound to fade. The three of us, attentive, watch him and wait. "I have something serious to discuss with you. You're a little young for this, Michael and Vicki, but you, Jo, are old enough."

Unexpected fear grips me. Though the air is warm, I feel a chill.

"This country's a goddam mess and it's going to get worse. It's bad enough living under this bloody racist Nationalist government, but things will be worse when it falls. By the turn of the century there'll be five million whites in this country and thirty million Blacks. You're not good at math, Joey, but you don't have to be to understand these numbers. One day there'll be a bloody revolution here: revenge, massacres, a bloodbath of whites that'll make Kenya and the Mau Mau look like a picnic. Goddammit. I thought we Jews were done running!"

My heart pounds so loudly I can hear it. Why is he telling us this? Who are the Mau Mau? Who will kill us? What have we done? Why must things change? What does he mean about Jews running?

"Don't think of this place as home. We'll have to leave and find home someplace not South Africa. You have to make yourself exportable."

He's looking at me, intense, unsmiling. Unusually, he seems to expect a response. Words tumble out of me: "Why can't we stay? I don't want to leave our house. Where will we go? When will we leave? Why will there be a bloodbath? Isn't this our country? Don't we belong? Will Granny and Grandpa come with us? You know Mommy will never leave them. She won't go."

His face clouds.

"Look around, Joey. Five million can't live at the expense of thirty million. Besides, I'm the paterfamilias. Your mother will do as I say."

I don't want to contradict him, but I *know* he's wrong on this one: My mother doesn't think he's the paterfamilias, and she doesn't do as he says. Still, it seems better not to tell him something I know he knows.

"Trust me, Joey. We have no choice. We *have* to leave. I'll figure out where we'll go. It won't happen soon. It requires planning. First, I have to make lots of money; second, I have to get that money out of this country so we can live someplace else the way we live here. All you have to do is make yourself *exportable*."

"What does exportable mean? How long will it take to make lots of money? How much is lots?"

Before I can ask any more questions, before he can answer those I've asked, my rod trembles, then arcs. A fish has taken the bait. I don't know what to do. My dad grabs my rod, lets out the line, reels it in, lets it out again, repeats the play, and eventually brings in the flapping, struggling fish, its scales iridescent and rainbow-hued in the bright Durban sun. I wish it were small so we'd have to throw it back, but it's big.

"Four pounds," my dad says, pulling out the hook and dropping the poor thing into our bucket. "Mmm," he says, "fried grunter for supper."

He's happy, but all I can think about is the bloody revolution, not getting killed, and not being home.

And what do we do with the fish? My mother will be annoyed if we bring it home in a bucket for the servants to clean. Though we've gone fishing more times than I can count, my dad has never figured out how to gut and scale. He always finds someone nearby to do us the favor.

A short distance down the quay, in the next gap between berthed vessels, an Indian man has been fishing all afternoon, watching four rods that look homemade. I've been watching him: his delicate, thin frame, his frequent checking and rechecking of his lines and bait. I know from my history book that Indians were first brought to South Africa in the 1860s as indentured laborers to work the sugar plantations and were treated badly. It's one hundred years later and he looks as though life still treats him badly.

My father tells us he will offer the man a few shillings to clean our fish and then our mother won't be annoyed, and Miriam, our cook, will make us delicious fried grunter for dinner.

We walk over with our fish in a bucket. My father, eager to engage in fisherman's banter, glances into the man's bucket. I look too. His bucket is empty. From his clothing and hollow eyes, we know he's there to bring home dinner to his family and not, as we, to while away the afternoon in search of wisdom about hills and valleys, bloodbaths, being exportable, and finding home someplace else.

I hope my father will not ask the man to clean our fish.

My father tells the man he would do us a great favor if he took our fish. The man, surprised, does us the favor. We thank him. I feel a rush of love for my father and know that from such a man all words are true. If he says we have to leave, we do; if he says home's not here, then it isn't. But I wish he'd tell me where it is.

2

Jewish Men Running: Three Portraits

MY "RUNNING" GRANDPARENTS WERE PART OF AN EPIC MOVEment of Jews fleeing persecution and poverty in Eastern Europe—over two and a half million between 1881 and 1924. Denied full citizen's rights in their natal countries, they were in search of "home"—a place of security, belonging, and freedom where they could raise their children without fear. They came from the Pale of Settlement—a large crescent of territory on the western margin of Russia to which Jews were confined by Tsarist decree after the partition of Poland between Prussia, Russia, and Austria in the late eighteenth century. Most moved to the United States. A smaller contingent made their way to South Africa, increasing the Jewish population from 4,000 in 1880 to more than 40,000 by 1914.

My paternal grandfather Joseph arrived in 1893. My maternal grandfather Sydney Orlin came in 1912. Each made a deep impact on me, and I am compelled to tell their stories and unpack the ways they affected mine.

But first, some words about South Africa and its Jews.

South Africa, like every diaspora, was not free from anti-Semitism. Its worst manifestations came from the apartheid-driving Nationalist Party, many of whose leaders in the 1930s identified with the Nazi movement. In 1930 Dr. D. F. Malan, who later served as prime minister from 1948 to 1954, introduced the Quota Act, effectively restricting Jewish immigration, arguing that Jews were an "unassimilable minority"; the Quota Act was followed by the Aliens Act of 1937, reinforcing the barrier against Jews at a time when they were desperate to find countries that would take them. The architect/father of apartheid and white supremacy legislation, Hendrick Verwoerd, prime minister from 1958 to 1966, was an unabashed Nazi sympathizer. For example, during his tenure as editor of the right-wing Afrikaner newspaper *Die Transvaler* (1937 to the early 1940s), he triumphantly headlined every Nazi victory during World War II as a strike against "British Jewish liberalism." He was succeeded by his mentee, John Vorster, prime minister from 1966 to 1978. Like his predecessor, Vorster was ardently pro-Nazi. Under his leadership, the Nationalist Party implemented apartheid legislation on a massive scale. Ironically, perhaps, as the Nationalist Party sought to increase the tally of its white citizenry, it became more willing to overlook the Jewish alienness of its Litvak population because their skin was, after all, white.

Portrait #1:
Paternal Grandfather Joseph: A Memoir in Midrashim

I never met my paternal grandfather Joseph; he died two years before I was born. I nonetheless have a relationship with him because absence is not nothing. For me, Joseph's absence was an ache, a longing filled with grief and desire—feelings that began when I was a little girl and that led me, as an adult, to search for him.

I first became aware of his absence on a family trip to visit my paternal grandmother, Bella, in the small country town of George in the Western Cape, where my father had grown up and Bella continued to live for many years after Joseph's death. I remember the moment: standing beside my father on Main Street facing a country store with a long stoep, above which, in large letters, was the name *J. Berelowitz & Sons*. My initial and surname.

Why, I wondered, did a country store two days' drive from our home in Durban have my name, and why did someone add *& Sons* when I was only six years old and had no sons?

My father, who knew everything, had the answer.

"Your grandfather's name was Joseph. It was his store. He added *& Sons* when your Uncle Sonny and I started working there. He thought we'd take it over when he died, but I hated small town life and left as soon as I could. Uncle Sonny stayed and never changed the sign. We named you after him: Joseph/Jo-Anne. It's not your store, though it's your initial and name."

I didn't, then, know the Ashkenazi custom of naming a child after a deceased relative—to honor the deceased, to keep their memory alive, to inspire the child to live up to her namesake's qualities, to pass on the ancient Jewish creed that memory is a moral imperative and that the self is bound into history. I didn't know the custom, but the instant I learned I was named for my grandfather, a shiver passed through me, so that I knew—intuitively—everything the ancient custom is meant to convey.

Zikhrono livrakha! May his memory be a blessing!

But how could I remember someone I never knew and of whom my father rarely spoke, though over the years I pressed him relentlessly for information? Over time, I stopped pressing. The ache of my namesake's absence dulled but never went away.

In the 1990s, when my father was in his eighties and more focused on the past than he had been, he handed me a manuscript on thin typewriter paper. The title: "A Family History."

"Here," he said. "You used to pester me about my father. Here's everything I remember."

The manuscript is brief, only twenty pages, odd for a man who loved language and never lost an opportunity to expatiate and hold an audience. Still, I was hopeful that treasure lay within. It held nuggets, things I hadn't known, like the names of the Lithuanian towns where Joseph and Bella were born, their separate emigrations to South Africa, the places each settled, their union, and stories about my father's childhood. But the treasure I'd hoped for wasn't there.

Though Bella was a presence, Joseph was a mere shadow.

Frustrated, I reread the manuscript—twice, thrice, four times—as though repeated readings might reveal text hidden behind my father's brief account. But the more I read, the more Joseph slipped through the lines. When I asked my father for more, for something solid, for memories he might pass on to me, he responded irritably, "It's *there*, everything I remember."

I wished I had another source, someone to challenge or cast light on my father's terse account. But there was no one left to ask. My father's longevity was an anomaly; his brothers died in their fifties: Sonny, the oldest, in 1971 of a heart attack on the luxury Blue Train between Cape Town and Pretoria; Reuben, the youngest, in the early 1980s.

I annoyed my father with my persistent questioning, annoyed myself for persisting when I already knew his answer.

"Joey, I don't know what to tell you. My father was a quiet man. Distant. He never said much, and I never asked him. I don't know why. He was my father. I took him for granted and never gave much thought to his life."

His response felt obdurate, though I've come, over the years, to accept it as his truth. Still, our different approaches to Joseph became one more issue between us. From my childhood into my thirties, I'd kept my father—my adored parent—on a pedestal, but as I grew into my own thoughts and opinions, I dislodged him and set him down on the dusty ground. The process was painful for both of us. Over time I came to regard our tensions over Joseph as symptomatic of something bigger: my father's rejection of his Jewish heritage—of his past—and my own evolving opposite move to engage with Jewish history and practice.

For a while, busy with my own life, I shelved my annoyance with my father's thin history and my obsession with the grandfather I longed to know more of. Time passed, and I might have let Joseph go were it not for a file my mother thrust at me one Sunday in 2017 when, as usual on a Sunday, I visited my parents—Father then ninety-eight, Mother, ninety—in their La Jolla, California, apartment.

"Here," my mother said, "take this. I've been throwing away rubbish. God knows why your father hung on to this. I was going to dump it, but I thought you might want it. You like old things. It's a speech Buthelezi gave to the South African Houses of Parliament. He gave Dad a copy."

I hesitated, reluctant to add to my own growing pile of papers, then reached for the old, scuffed black file. I had no affection for Mangosuthu Gatsha Buthelezi, the Zulu tribal chieftain who founded the Inkathata Freedom Party in 1975. Though seeming to oppose the apartheid government, he became a collaborator and puppet and gave testimony that helped convict Black activists.

In 1975, when his star was ascending and it seemed he might challenge Mandela's role as leader of Black South Africa, he and my father, by pure chance, spent two weeks together at a luxury health spa outside Cape Town. My father was at the spa in search of relief from debilitating arthritis; I don't know Buthelezi's reason. What I do know is that my father delighted in the novelty of sharing steam baths, high colonics, cleansing fasts, lymphatic massages, and zero calorie food with a man South Africa's racial laws proscribed him from engaging with except within the structures and strictures of South Africa's apartheid regime.

What none of us realized was that Buthelezi's presence at the health spa, his "honorary white status"—a term the apartheid government borrowed from the Nazis who conferred "honorary Aryan" on their Japanese allies—was a sign of collaboration with the apartheid government.

I brought the file home, placed it on my desk, and tried to get on with other tasks. But I couldn't. The file was like a magnet and I some kind of ferric matter irresistibly drawn to it. Repeatedly, my hand reached toward it, and my gaze, though I willed it not to, fixed on its worn surface, so that, at last, surrendering, I opened it. I reckoned I'd speed-read my way through Buthelezi's speech, confirm my dismissive preconceptions of him, dump it into our recycling bin, and thereby free myself from whatever strange charge the file exerted.

My preconceptions were right: There was nothing in the speech I wanted, and so I unhooked the pages from their metal clasps. And then I froze. At the back of the file, behind Buthelezi's speech, lay a legal-sized document, foxed, with reddish-brown signs of aging, creased and sepia-toned, two holes punched into the left side, the edges of the punch holes rusty from the iron fastener. A certificate, it bore a date, 1903, and, in cursive writing, a name, Joseph Berelowitz.

It was my grandfather's certificate of naturalization, the official document granting him full rights as a citizen in the Colony of the Cape of Good Hope.

So much painful history sandwiched between the covers of that file! An African denied rights in the country of his birth; a Jew denied rights in Lithuania, the country of his birth, but granted them in South Africa, the land to which he'd come in search of freedom.

Awed, I lifted the paper from the iron fastener and gazed upon it, gazed *through* it to a moment 114 years ago when Joseph, three times, signed his name:

> Whereas Joseph Berelowitz . . . And whereas the said Joseph Berelowitz . . . Joseph Berelowitz shall henceforth . . . be deemed . . . to be entitled to all political and other rights, powers, and privileges, and be subject to all obligations to which a natural born British subject is entitled or subject in this Colony.

Reverently, I touched the letters, tracing Joseph's careful cursive, my fingers echoing the movement of his pen as he wrote his name, a name I hold in mine, a name I have been charged to make a blessing of.

My mother, having deemed the file *rubbish*, would have thrown it away. But once I discovered it held something precious, I felt bound to inquire if my father would like it back.

"Dad, this was in the file Mom gave me. Do you want it?"

"I don't remember ever seeing it," said my father. "I don't have any use for it. If you want it, it's yours."

"Dad, there's something else." I showed him that the dates and information in his "Family History" didn't match the information in the document. He'd written that his father was sixteen when he came to South Africa. But according to the certificate in my hand, he was twenty-three in 1903 and had been living in the Colony for nine years and eleven months. If he was twenty-three in 1903 and was, as my father wrote, born in 1880, he'd have been thirteen, not sixteen, when he left Lithuania and came to South Africa.

"Oh Joey, I don't know. I thought he told me he was sixteen. He never said much and I never asked him. He was a distant man. I took him for granted."

Had I made a mistake? Had my poor math skills misled me? I went back to my father's "Family History" and read again that his father was born in 1880 in the Pale of Settlement in the Lithuanian province of Kovno in the town of Shavil and that he emigrated when he was sixteen to avoid conscription into the brutal Russian army.

Which was true? Was Joseph thirteen or sixteen when, in 1893, he docked in Cape Town's harbor and made his way across the country to the mining town of Johannesburg? I chose thirteen. Chose it because my father's memory was faulty, because he seemed to know so little about Joseph, because he always emphasized Joseph's probity and the document bears Joseph's signature, and because a boy of thirteen traveling alone from Lithuania to South Africa is a more compelling story.

But how would I track his journey? How to fill the silent spaces of a distant man who never said much?

The library, books, articles. My skills as a research scholar would help me fill in the gaps.

In March 1881, a year after Joseph's birth, members of a Russian revolutionary group assassinated Tsar Alexander II with a bomb on a street in St. Petersburg. The group included a Jewish woman who provided shelter for her fellow conspirators. News of Jewish involvement in the assassination unleashed a wave of anti-Jewish rioting, pillaging, rape, and pogroms throughout southern Russia and Ukraine. The assassination led to even more draconian limits than those already governing Jewish life; the near-starving Jewish population grew desperate; the trickle of Jews who had begun leaving the Russian/Lithuanian Pale of Settlement in the 1860s turned into a flood.

Most of the 40,000 who came to South Africa were from the province of Kovno, many from Shavil. Ninety percent were between fourteen and forty-four, though some were younger. Between 1904 and 1906, the years following Joseph's naturalization, 1,237 Litvaks applied for naturalization in the Cape Colony, among them 428 "general dealers"—the profession Joseph listed on his certificate.

Eagerly I read, burrowing my way into the past, trying to situate Joseph within this flood of emigrants. In 1893 it was extremely difficult for Jews to leave the Pale of Settlement. How did a boy of thirteen negotiate the network of illegal agents selling information about trains, desirable routes, porous areas along the German border, and the names of contacts in port cities like Libau, Hamburg, Bremen, Amsterdam, and Rotterdam?

I learned that Jews could, in one of those cities, purchase a voucher to Cape Town, but they would have to get to London to use it. Once there, they would likely have stayed in London's East End, in the Poor Jews' Temporary Shelter, a refuge offering protection from crooked shipping agents, larcenous porters, and greedy lodging-house keepers. After about fourteen days, voucher in hand, the emigrant would have been put on a train to Southampton and thence on a ship owned by the Union-Castle Line, whose advertisements proclaimed, "Best Route to the Goldfields."

But the more research I did, the more Joseph withdrew into the shadows. I lost him in the great sweep of historical forces drawing desperadoes and dreamers to distant lands. Frustrated, I closed my books and turned back to my father's "Family History." There, though shadowy, Joseph was still a singular presence. I needed to find a way to hold on to that presence, to the singularity of that boy of thirteen who became my grandfather.

And then it occurred to me that I had another resource, one outside my training as a scholar, though I had been exposed to it: a practice within Judaism known as midrash.

The Torah is filled with stories, many of them laconic descriptions of dramatic events, flash narratives that stimulate a reader's desire for the "what next?" and "how does it end?" so integral to humankind's engagement with story. What, for example, did Sarah feel when Abraham set off with her only son, Isaac, whom she loved, to sacrifice him as a burnt offering on Mount Moriah? What happened to Dinah after Shechem raped her and her brothers killed the men of Shechem? The Bible never answers these questions. But readers long to know.

To fill this need, rabbis invented stories, midrashim, supplemental accounts that answer our human longing to know more. Although they're inventions, midrashim try to stay true to the characters in the canonical text. Supplemental narratives, they seem to bubble up into the empty spaces of the primary text, or to lie *behind* the given text, waiting for an opportunity to emerge.

I could, I realized, switch out of my mode of scholar-searching-for-hard-data to something more rabbinic, more midrashic; I could invent stories to fill the holes in my father's porous account; I could allow imagination to answer my longing for stories about my grandfather.

But first I had to *see* him; I needed anecdote and description, something *visual* to create my fuller picture. And because I wanted to root my midrash in reality, I needed *cues*.

I had them. My father gave them to me. It took me a while to recognize their richness because they're rough, bare outlines, odd bits of information scattered throughout my father's terse account, small flashes of illumination casting light onto shadow.

"Afrikaner farmers," my father wrote, "called my father the *Rooi Jood*, the Red Jew, because his hair was red." A little further on: "My father was so strong he could throw a bale of hay onto the back of a wagon; he was so fearless he went into a stable of horses to separate two stallions who were fighting."

A bale of hay, I learned from Google, can weigh four hundred pounds. And stallions, I learned from watching YouTube videos, are fierce and terrifying fighters.

Joseph became, for me, a red-haired, Yiddish-speaking John Henry.

Beside that (mythical) image, I placed my father: five-foot-eight, dark-haired, physically clumsy, literate, verbally dexterous.

Did ever a father and son have so little in common?

My father wrote:

"Johannesburg was the cesspool of the world, too much for my father's incongruously puritan character."

Rich material for a midrash.

I closed my eyes and imagined young Joseph stepping off the train into Johannesburg's Market Square after a sixty-hour journey from Cape Town:

On his long passage from Shavil to London, on his ocean voyage from Southampton to Cape Town, on his train ride from Cape Town to Johannesburg, my young grandfather-to-be dreams of a land without Cossacks, a land without pogroms, a pastoral paradise, an African Eden, eternally warm, bathed in golden light, a peaceful kingdom of exotic animals, a New Jerusalem in a virgin land, streets paved in gold, rivers of milk and honey, a promised land of meek and righteous souls who love justice. Alone on those long journeys—though always surrounded by strangers—he dreams dreams of deliverance like those of the ancient prayer: "May there be abundant peace from heaven and a good life for all."

He steps off the train.

What is this godless place?

Amid the surging crowd, young Joseph stands, a boy-man with a mop of red hair and a strong physique, a Litvak John Henry. In shock, immobile, he stands. Before him, a scene of iniquity: haggling, cursing, fighting, men and women buying and selling everything from heavy mining machinery to fresh produce to favors; a melee of one hundred outspanned wagons offloading goods and people—more people than he'd ever beheld in Shavil, even on the busiest market day; people more different than he'd imagined walked this earth: Indians from the sugarcane fields of Natal, Zulus from the coastal lowlands, Xhosas from the Eastern Cape, artisans and miners from the gold and silver mines of the Americas and Australia, coal and tin miners from Europe, solicitors, engineers, pimps, adventurers, crooks, and philanderers from everywhere.

This place is Babylon.

A woman grabs his jacket, pulls him to her, her breath rank as she whispers obscenities, words he's never heard before, in a language he doesn't know but instinctively understands—her personal invitation to Sodom and Gomorrah. She shifts to Yiddish, and his bile rises at a fellow Jew sunk so low in this filthy mire. Swallowing his vomit, he pulls back, shakes her off, turns from Babylon, climbs back onto the train, finds a seat whose window shade is drawn against the bright Highveld sunlight, against the abomination of Market Square. He waits for night to fall and the train to pull out and make its slow way to the next station, and the next and the next. It is headed back to Cape Town, but he will find a stopping point along the way, somewhere remote, someplace not a city.

When Johannesburg is two days' travel behind him and the country open and wide, the train stops at a small station. It's not really a station, for there's nothing there, nothing to mark it save for a sign on a transverse wooden plank nailed to an upright beam. The sign reads Rondevlei.

The man in the seat beside him rises and lifts his bag from the rack above. Perhaps he knows this Rondevlei? In a pidgin mix of Yiddish and Afrikaans, Joseph asks, "Iz dort werk hier?" *Is there work here?*

"Ja, as jy met perde werk en perde breek?" *Yes, if you work with horses and break horses.*

"Dankie meneer. Ikh sal hier blayben." *Thank you, sir. I will stay here.*

For the next twenty-three years, Joseph lives in Rondevlei.

Again, I returned to my father's manuscript—my ur-text, my source.

My father wrote: "My father left Johannesburg to live in—of all places—a small village called Rondevlei, a godforsaken place where a lot of impoverished Afrikaans farmers eked out some kind of living."

Godforsaken.

My father wrote and spoke this word each time he mentioned Rondevlei. He spoke it with contempt—his lips grimacing, his stomach clenching, his spine recoiling into his chairback—as though Rondevlei were an affront. I imagined him typing the word with the same physical revulsion, his arthritic fingers recoiling from the keyboard with each strike. Rondevlei as epithet. Rondevlei as godforsakenness.

Godforsaken Rondevlei became, for me, as essential to Joseph as his red hair, his fearlessness, and his strength. The very word conjured for me an arid landscape of dry scrub, thorn bush, and bleached rock, the South African version of the Azazel of Leviticus 16:22: "a land cut off." Joseph must have settled, I thought, in the Karoo, a semidesert the size of Germany, whose name, Karoo, is Koi-San for "dry place." In my mind's eye I saw my grandfather in dun-colored clothing in a dun-colored landscape, his only companion his shadow in an endless vista of dun relieved only by the red flame of his hair.

Under cloudless skies, Joseph breathes hot, dry air in summer and cold, dry air in winter. Alone at night, he gazes up at a dark sky. In summer, he sees Orion, Perseus, and the Great Bear; in winter, gleaming Scorpio, Hercules, and Sagittarius; in autumn, Leo and Hydra; in the spring, Andromeda, Aquarius, and Perseus; and always, in every season, the Southern Cross and Centaurus circling the South Pole.

He has traveled a great distance. Distance is his companion.

Above: vastness. Below: Joseph, solitary, "in a godforsaken place where," as his future son will write, "impoverished Afrikaner farmers eke out a meager living."

In the early days he breaks horses for poor farmers, training them not to rear, to wear and respond to a bit, to pull in a team, to be ridden. At some point, he opens a small store, a klein winkel, *a shed really, with a corrugated iron roof and mud walls, where he sells dry goods purchased from Jewish wholesalers in nearby Oudtshoorn: grain feed, flour, small ploughs, bridles, rope, tobacco, yards of cloth, and, as though in mitigation, small hard candies.*

Dry goods for dry folk, dour Calvinists who cling to the harsh doctrines of the Dutch Reformed Church; their only respite from the daily scrabble of existence the dominee's Sunday sermon, followed, perhaps, by a special Sabbath indulgence of sticky braided koeksisters tart with lemon and sharp with ginger, or a rusk spread with homemade fig jam, and, for the children, small hard candies from the Rooi Jood's store.

Though my father's manuscript made little reference to history, he noted that in 1899 the Second Anglo-Boer War broke out. There was fighting in the Western Cape where Joseph had settled; the British built garrisons there, imprisoned and killed many Boers.

A British commander, suspicious of a young Jew living among Afrikaners, arrested and interrogated Joseph on charges of spying; finding nothing, the commander let him go. The war raged until 1902. Able-bodied men became scarce and Afrikaner women, widowed early, struggled to maintain difficult farmland.

Again, my father: "He broke horses and opened a small store and lived alone in that godforsaken place until 1916 . . . and I assure you he was celibate for he was rigidly moral and refused to compromise himself with any of the Afrikaner women in Rondevlei."

For my father, Joseph's celibacy was a matter of rigid morality, a refusal to compromise. I was less certain. Why would a young, strong man choose to be celibate for twenty-three years?

"Dad, I don't think it was necessarily Joseph's choice to be celibate. I suspect he didn't have a choice, for I can't imagine an Afrikaner family permitting a daughter to consort with a Jew."

"You're wrong, Joey. My father was a good-looking man and strong. Afrikaner women would have wanted to marry him."

A young Afrikaner huisvrou, *recently informed of her husband's death in a guerilla skirmish with the British, sleeps alone in her four-poster bed carved from local stinkwood. The farm is now her responsibility, hers alone—too much for a single woman whose domain is the kitchen, not the land and the harvest and the horses. One night the* Rooi Jood *appears to her in a dream: she sees his red hair, his strong back, the effortless way he throws a bale of hay onto a wagon. Night after night she dreams of him. Alone in bed she tosses, remembering a time when she'd watched him mount a neighbor's difficult colt. He'd gripped its flanks with his knees, bent his red head over its russet mane, ridden him hard toward the purple-peaked Swartberg mountains, returned, dismounted, and caressed the subdued animal. Alone in her bed, she caresses her body and her hair, dreaming that the hand on her body and in her hair is the* Rooi Jood's, *that the hair in her hand is his red flame.*

The following day she walks to his store to purchase flour, nails, and horse feed. The Rooi Jood *bends to retrieve a bag of nails from a shelf below the counter. Her hands twitch in longing to reach out and touch his fire. Over the next few days, her waking hours enriched by dreams from the previous night, she finds other reasons to return, other goods she needs. One morning, compelled by a longing she cannot resist, she takes from her pantry two mason jars of fig jam made last summer from figs so ripe that nectar oozed from their stems, sweetness so precious she'd preserved it and laid it by for her husband's return. But her husband is dead, killed by the British, and the* Rooi Jood *is here, alive, with no woman to sweeten his nights.*

She stands in the winkel's *doorway. The* Rooi Jood, *courteous, greets her.*

"Goeie more, mevrou. Hoe kan ik jou help?" *Good morning, madam. How may I help you?*

"Ek het jou konfyt gebring, iets soet." *I brought you fig jam, something sweet.*

Shyly, she pushes the jam across the counter.

"Dankie, maar ek het nie soet konfyt nodig nie." *Thank you, but I don't need sweet fig jam.*

He pushes it back across the counter and pulls back.

Distance is his companion.

I google Rondevlei.

It isn't in the Karoo.

The word means "round marsh," and it's not the name of a town, though it might once have been. Rondevlei is now the name of a nature preserve, a protected wetland of international importance comprising three distinct marshes: the Elandvlei, the Langvlei, and the Rondevlei, with 230 different species of bird, including the kingfisher, the grey heron, the little egret, the brightly feathered knysna loerie, flamingoes, pelicans, African fish eagles, marsh harriers, and hook-billed shrikes. Small mammals abound: the cape clawless otter, the cape grey mongoose, moles, shrews, badgers, mice, monkeys, porcupines, angulate tortoises, the Cape dwarf chameleon. There is even a population of hippos. Until 1919, when local farmers exterminated them, the nearby forests of Tsitsikamma supported herds of African bush elephants. The lakes are so abundant in fish—big lervis, black bass, blue kurper, grunter, Cape moonies, mullet, and springers—that a light beamed into the water at night makes them jump, shimmering and iridescent, into a fisherman's boat, with no need to cast a line. Abundant native flora include the Cape Flats conebush, the Cape Flats dune strandveld, lowveld fynbos, proteas, and heathers. Giant rain spiders weave silk threads to trap lizards and dragonflies, and the air is filled with birdsong.

"Dad," I asked, "why have you always described Rondevlei as 'godforsaken'? It seems more like paradise."

"Because it *was* godforsaken. It was in the middle of nowhere. Nothing there. No one. Just a bunch of poor Afrikaners."

"Why do you think your father made his home in a godforsaken place with poor Afrikaners for twenty-three years?"

"I don't know, Joey. He was a quiet man. Distant. He never said much, and I never asked him."

He is, in his way, comfortable with these Afrikaners. Though he is, to them, an outsider, a Jew, he finds their world and their lives familiar. Their piety, poverty, clannishness, their outcast status in the British Empire, remind him of his village in the old country where Jews were even poorer than these Afrikaners and even more despised. There, Poles and Russians regarded Jews as vermin; here, it's the British who show contempt, who regard Afrikaners as brutish oafs. In one respect, the British are correct: Afrikaners behave brutishly to Africans and Coloreds, but so, beneath their veneer, do the British, who condescend to everyone—Jew, Afrikaner, Black, Colored, Indian—to everyone not British.

He could, if he wanted the company of fellow Jews, move twelve miles to Oudtshoorn, the Little Jerusalem of Africa, where a third of the white citizenry are Litvaks, many from Shavil. But prosperous Oudtshoorn, capital of the ostrich feather business, is not for him. He does not like these ostrich men, with their fancy talk about foreign markets and exotic plumes and fashion trends and stock exchanges and trade and wholesalers and supply and demand and investors in Trieste and London and Morocco and Paris and New York. Better to live among these dour Afrikaners. At least they leave him alone.

"Dad," I pushed on, relentless, "your father must have liked his solitary life in Rondevlei to have stayed so long. Why do you think he gave it up for marriage?"

"I don't know, Joey. Perhaps he was tired. Perhaps he couldn't resist pressure from my mother. She was a driving force—outgoing, needing and wanting people."

Over the years, Joseph's red hair fades. By 1916, when he stands under the chuppah with young Bella, a yarmulke covering the thinning crown of his head, he is a gray-haired man, though sunlight picks up whispers of reddish ginger. Bella is tall, strong-limbed, dark-haired, aglow with her own fire, determined he and she will not remain in Rondevlei, though Joseph tells her it is paradise and he would prefer to stay. But for Bella it is too small, too isolated, and there are no Jews there. And so, the newlyweds move to George, a pretty town of 6,000 where twelve Jewish families have settled.

On the wall outside my father's office in my parents' La Jolla apartment, there once hung two framed photographs that captured my grandparents at this moment in their lives.

The photographs have a new home now: the wall adjacent to my desk. Frequently I remove them from the wall and place them *on* my desk, as though their physical proximity could trigger some new insight. To further reduce the distance, I lift first one, then the other, almost to my nose, myopically staring into their faded realities, willing them to yield their secrets. But they refuse.

They're clearly taken by a professional, formal and official looking. My father thought they were taken at the behest of a *shadchan*—a professional matchmaker who would have required them as part of the matchmaking process—a first step for clients seeking a marriage partner.

I try to imagine Joseph and Bella each staring at the other's photograph.

Who is this person? Is he/she kind? Can love bloom with this stranger? Can we build a life together?

Joseph looks to be about thirty-six, his age when he married Bella. He's dressed in a three-piece suit—attire for courtship, not horse-breaking or the operation of a small country store. His outfit

Joseph Berelowitz.

was, I suspect, provided by the photographer, for other details are clearly studio props: the small patch of carpet on which Joseph stands, the swag of drapery behind him, the Doric column, its capital partly obscured by a great froth of artificial vines, the small table at his right on which he's set his hat, turned to show the ribbon on the hatband, the elegant cane on which he rests his hand.

I imagine the photographer arranging him, telling him to place his feet just so: in a slight contrapposto—weight on his left leg, the right slightly bent at the knee, a studied asymmetry to lend relaxation to his client's shy and stiff demeanor.

Bella's photograph shows a smooth-skinned woman about eighteen years old—her age when she married Joseph. She's dressed in white, in a kind of pinafore cinched under the generous curve of her bosom. Her hair is carefully coiffed, probably permed. In her face I see my father's: the firm jaw tilted up, the expression of determination, the prominent nose, the direct gaze; but unlike my father, her lips are full and soft. Her right arm is in shadow, so I focus on her left—its sleeve rolled up to the elbow crease to reveal a forearm muscular and capable, its nakedness almost shocking. More than her determined face, it's her bare arm that holds my gaze. Was Joseph, like me, riveted by that arm, by its promise of youthful strength?

I didn't accept my father's line that Joseph married because "he was tired." What seemed more likely was that the distant relatives who took Bella in when she arrived from Lithuania set out to find her a Jewish husband—and the sooner the better. Pickings were probably slim; Joseph may have been the only Jewish bachelor for many miles. Perhaps the *shadchan* and Bella's relatives sought to remind him that marriage, in Judaism, is a mitzvah, part of God's covenant with Abraham: *Be fruitful and multiply*. Perhaps, at thirty-six, Joseph felt an obligation to marry.

On second thought, perhaps my father was right: Joseph *was* tired.

My father was certainly right about Bella: She was a driving

Bella Berelowitz.

force. Determined to create a nucleus of Jews in Afrikaner Calvinist George, Bella journeyed to Port Elizabeth, two hundred miles away, to lobby Jewish merchants for money to build a synagogue in George. Through her efforts, the small Jewish community grew—a little. Taking under her wing Jewish newcomers, she welcomed them to her Shabbat table—of which my father wrote with more detail and pleasure than any memories he rendered of Joseph: chicken soup and huge, meaty pierogen, followed by fried sole and gefilte fish, or sometimes a whole baked fish, then roast chicken with potatoes crisped to a quarter inch of crust; for dessert, baked apples and local hanepoot-muscat grapes from Calitzdorp across the mountains.

Though literate only in Yiddish, Bella was determined to enhance the opportunities of the three sons she bore Joseph: Sonny, my father Morris Abraham, and Reuben. To that end, she organized an annual fundraiser for their school, taking personal charge of the sweet stall, which glistened with home-baked honeyed delights and iridescent mason jars of fig and watermelon konfyt. Working tirelessly beside Joseph in the store—those strong arms!—she helped make the little business prosper, and soon it grew from a shed behind their house to an address on Main Street with a raised stoep for displaying goods. A large sign proudly announced the name: *J Berelowitz*.

Through Bella, Joseph reentered Jewish life and became part of the Jewish community. Every Passover, according to my father, he bought a crate of sweet red grapes from Worcester in the Breede River Valley, where hot summers concentrate grape sugars; from them he made a barrel of sweet wine he decanted into bottles for the bank manager, the headmaster, and the doctor. Too shy to bear the gifts himself, he dispatched my father to deliver them, together with packages of Bella's homemade matzoh. Though not ordinarily a singing man, on the High Holy Days, according to my father, Joseph sang liturgical melodies, those ancient, plangent songs that fill Jewish hearts through the Days of Awe. Perhaps he harkened to a mystic echo from the great cantors of Kovno, near Shavil, where Jewish voices resonated for centuries through the narrow streets, praising God and imploring Him to inscribe them for another year in the Book of Life. Perhaps those ancient rhythms of Jewish journeys—exodus, exile, diaspora, and homecoming—burst from Joseph's soul, bringing forth songs dormant for the twenty-three years he'd removed himself from Jewish life. Perhaps Bella's love inspired him to reach his baritone to those distant places whence he and she had journeyed, so that he filled the little house in George with unaccustomed sound, pouring out his longing for a world redeemed from suffering and transformed into a kingdom of universal peace.

To Bella he surrendered the task of bringing up the boys, but on weekends and after school they helped him in the store, attending to his warning, in Yiddish, to *gib Achtung,* pay attention, lest someone steal. Once a month on a Sunday morning my father would help Joseph check the account books to make sure that all was in order and that everyone to whom money was due had received it. On summer evenings when the days were long, and on Sundays when the shop was shuttered, Joseph farmed their four-acre lot, tending to his corn, sunflowers, vegetable beds, and fruit trees. No longer living in a natural paradise, he cultivated one—always, according to my father, alone, never teaching his boys to garden, never soliciting their assistance.

Distance remained his companion, for though his life had changed, Joseph was still silent and solitary. Again, my father: "He was a loner, a shy man, distant." I wondered if my father's compulsive repetition of Joseph's distance helped dull the aching pain of a remote father.

The boys grew to manhood. Sonny and my father worked with Joseph in the store. Joseph added *& Sons* to the sign above the stoep. World War II broke out. Sonny and Reuben enlisted with the British army.

Once 32,000 Jews lived in Joseph's home province of Kovno—23 percent of Kovno's population. From June 1940 to June 1941, the Soviet army occupied the city of Kovno. They exiled to Siberia Jews they suspected of capitalist or bourgeois nationalist activities. In June 1941, the Nazis arrived. Armed Lithuanian thugs carried out bloody attacks on Jews, hunting them down and killing them. The Nazis removed the remaining 30,000 Jews to the old ghetto, built to house 6,000, and sealed it. They took 9,000 to a tsarist-era fort, the Ninth Fort, where on November 25 and November 29 they murdered them. In October 1943 they transferred almost the entire remaining ghetto population to labor camps or murdered them in mass shootings. When the Soviet army arrived in August 1944, ninety Jews were left.

I asked my father how his father dealt with the tragedy of Kovno, with what happened to the Jews there. "He must have had family members who perished," I said.

"Oh, Joey, I don't know. He was a quiet man. I don't remember him saying anything about it. I don't remember him speaking about the war. My mother was the one who followed it. She was always listening to the radio, wanting news about Sonny and Reuben. If I remember correctly, my father would go after work to the bedroom where he kept a book by his bedside. He read it all the time."

That book, my father noted, "was *The Socialist Sixth of the World* by the Red Dean of Canterbury."

We learn about people from the books that sustain them. What, I wondered, would I learn about Joseph from reading a book he read "all the time"?

I checked out a copy from my university library.

The "Red Dean of Canterbury" was the nickname for Hewlitt Johnson, Dean of Canterbury, a Christian Marxist, who toured the Soviet Union in 1934 and 1937, recording his observations and publishing them in 1939 in *The Socialist Sixth of the World*. Johnson copied much of his text word for word from pro-Soviet propaganda produced by organizations such as the Society of Cultural Relations with the USSR, of which he was the chairperson. Members included E. M. Forster, Julian Huxley, Maynard Keynes, Bertrand Russell, Sybil Thorndyke, Alexei Tolstoy, and Virginia Woolf. I wondered if those illustrious authors wrote, or edited, the propaganda material that Johnson copied, for some of it is fine prose, though what the book describes is a utopic fantasy, more fairy tale than reportage, a dream world sustained by elegant prose.

Shy, solitary, distant, unable to bear the world's godforsakenness, unable to bear Bella's chronic anxiety about her absent sons, incapable of hovering with her each night beside the radio for news of the war, Joseph retreats into the dreamscape of Johnson's Socialist Sixth of the World. *In the silent night, his wife snoring softly beside him, he reads—reads and rereads—Johnson's paean to the redemptive new Soviet state:* "Dawn breaks over the east. And in that fresh dawn men see the promise of a new world, not a perfect world, and not a Utopian world, but at least a world freed from poverty and exploitation . . . where mankind . . . may find within itself a nobler and more enduring goodness and beauty."

This is what he has always longed for—a world of goodness and beauty where all mankind is, at last, Home. How strange that the world he fled has become paradise! Stirred by Johnson's words, he yearns for his old home, though he knows it is no more. Weary, caught between despair and hope, he shuts his precious book, turns off the light, closes his eyes, and dreams of the glorious socialist sixth of the world.

Historian Ruth Gay, in her book *Unfinished People*, describes Eastern European child immigrants like Joseph as hopeful, idealistic, unskilled, uneducated, and, above all, *unfinished*—no longer children, not yet adults, embarked on journeys they were too young to undertake and too undeveloped to process. Many child immigrants, Gay argues, never recovered from the aloneness and alienation of their experiences. To cope, they developed a quality of *reserve*.

Reserve is Ruth Gay's word. *Distant* was my father's. Though not synonyms, they overlap, for both carry a sense of emotional distance, of feelings checked, and absence of affect. But *distant*, at least in the context of my father's history, is more loaded, more poignant because it's *physical, spatial*. Reflecting on my father's almost compulsive repetition of the word, I recalled a story he once told me that brought home Joseph's emotional distance: "When I was eight or nine," he said, "my father journeyed to a faraway town for the funeral of a relative and was gone several days. When he returned, I ran to him, threw my arms about his legs and hugged him. He pushed me away so that I almost fell and said, '*Gay avek*,' go away."

Were there other equally painful memories my father chose to repress?

I've come to understand the shadowiness of his memories. It must have been impossible to get close to a father unable to overcome his own loneliness, incapable of tolerating closeness, who survived by remaining in the shadows and who, when his sons went to war, retreated into a book with a fairy-tale happy ending.

Have my midrashim done anything to make Joseph's memory a blessing? Or have I, in trying to fill the silent spaces of my father's history, created only noise, transgressing the injunction in the Book of Ecclesiastes: *Do not rush to speak; let your words be few*. Might I have better served Joseph and my father by sitting silently with their grief and mine?

Grief.

Perhaps that's the real issue here: my resistance to absence, emptiness, and silence—the nothingness that is humankind's destiny. For, in truth, though I am a quiet person—a trait I've surely inherited from Joseph—I don't want silence. I want the noise of answers, the cacophony of words creating bulwarks against the void. And so I write this memoir, this document of melancholia, compiled of ruins, fragments, supplements, distortions, and fictions, clinging tenaciously to the past—to my ancestors, to my youth, to the countries and traditions I'm both from and part of—searching for my place in the world, a place where I belong.

Portrait #2: Maternal Grandfather Sydney: A "Memoranda"

I knew my maternal grandfather, Sydney Orlin, well. He and Granny Rochel lived on our street, Musgrave Road, close enough that my nanny walked me there on Sundays so I could bake cookies and jam tarts with Granny for Grandpa's Sunday poker game; and I visited often with my mother, who adored her parents; additionally, they frequently came to our house in the late afternoon for tea or a glass of sherry so Grandpa could check on my father and inquire what orders had come in to the factory, which Grandpa founded in the 1920s and handed over to my father in 1951 because my mother begged him to get her out of George and home to Durban and would he please, please, give my father a chance—which Grandpa did—with misgivings, reluctantly.

In short, Grandpa Sydney was part of my childhood and adolescence. His age, then, spanned his late fifties into his early seventies—not, by today's standards, *old*; yet I always thought of him as old, though now I think he was prematurely worn down from the hard-driving life of his youthful adventuring, the malaria that ravaged his body when he was a young man, and the emphysema that gradually robbed his body of oxygen and turned his lungs into wet sponges. In any event, I always had difficulty reconciling the "old man" of my youth with Grandpa's tales of his youthful invincible masculinity. But I have a written document to support that invincible masculinity—Grandpa's memoir—and though he's the author and its tenor is unquestionably boosterish, I believe it to be true because it's too extraordinary for Grandpa to have invented and, besides, he wrote it as a legacy and moral lesson for his first grandson, my brother Michael, and Grandpa meant it as an exemplary tale.

It lies on my desk: a thirty-seven-page, typed document with editorial markings in blue ink, bound in a black file folder whose texture has so softened over the years that it feels like vellum.

Grandpa didn't call it a memoir; that word wasn't in his vocabulary. He called it a "memoranda"—a curious plural designation, more appropriate for a business or legal document than for an account of a life, but it's appropriate for Grandpa, who was, when he wrote it in the late 1960s, a businessman, more familiar with the terse concision of business writing than with the ruminative essaying that has marked memoir since Montaigne. "Memoranda," moreover, suggests brevity, notes, mnemonic aids for future use, information to be expanded upon—later. Does an imperative lurk there? *Remember! Do not forget, for I am your grandfather who begat you!* Perhaps. Or is it my melancholia, my longing to recuperate the past that leads me to think so? And my narcissism to think that I alone of Grandpa's seven grandchildren am qualified, by temperament and profession, to take up that charge, if there is one?

On second thought, memoranda is probably an appropriate word, for Grandpa's text reads as a chronology of adversities overcome and successes attained. Not surprisingly for a man whose education ended with his bar mitzvah, who wasn't a reader and had no understanding of conventions in literary genres, there's no narrative arc. Moreover, for me, a historian, the document tantalizes with rich passing references that Grandpa never unpacks—like South Africa's 1913 General Strike, in which unionized white mineworkers sought to exclude Black workers from positions of authority. In short, my attention is drawn as much by what Grandpa makes note of as by the lacunae that open out beneath his passing references.

I want to get in there, fill the empty spaces, and learn more about the grandfather I *thought* I knew.

Where shall I begin?

With the passage of his memoir/memoranda into my hands.

A Sunday morning, 2017. I'm visiting my parents, asking questions, as I usually do, about the past. On this visit, Grandpa's on my mind because the previous night I'd watched *Tim's Vermeer*, a documentary about a technology entrepreneur who attempted to replicate Vermeer's photographically realistic style. Vermeer always makes me think of Grandpa for reasons that will soon become clear, but the trigger that kept my mind on Grandpa that Sunday visit was an object on my mother's coffee table—a ceramic plate with a decoupage photo of my siblings and me from the early 1960s. Grandpa had it made when he visited Japan, and we'd all found it extraordinary, a testament to Japanese ingenuity, though it struck me then—now too—as odd to put loved ones' faces on a dinner plate. I reach forward and pick it up—not from any interest in the plate but because it connects me to Grandpa, prompting a question I'd long wanted to ask about Grandpa's trip to Japan so many decades ago.

"I've always wondered," I say, "if Grandpa slept with a geisha. He seemed to have a special twinkle in his eyes when he told us about geishas. And Granny didn't go with him, so he could easily have done so."

My parents exchange glances. "I wouldn't be one bit surprised," my mother says, "and she wouldn't have been the first. Grandpa had lots of affairs. There was a woman who worked at Anstey's, the department store; he maintained her in a flat in the building he owned next door, and he'd have Johannes, his African driver, wait outside in the car when he went in for a quickie. I know there were others."

I'm astonished—and almost perversely pleased to learn that Gramps stayed lusty into his senior years. Granny's devotion to him was doglike; impossible to think of her ever being his sexual partner, though two stillborn sons and two living daughters testify that she was, four times at least.

"Did Granny know? How did you know?"

"I don't know if she knew. Probably. I don't think she'd have cared, as long as he stayed with her. Dad and I know because someone blackmailed Grandpa about it, a man who lived in the building; a slimy fellow, according to Grandpa. Grandpa told him to rot in hell before he'd pay him a penny."

"He regretted that when he was dying," my father adds. "Grandpa was superstitious. He thought the blackmailer had put a hex on him and that's why he was dying."

I shake my head, attempting to reconfigure my image of Grandpa, a picture that's now unhinged and scrambled. Headshaking doesn't help.

"Grandpa wrote an autobiography," my mother says. "Don't you remember? He wrote it for Michael after Michael asked him how he started the factory. I don't remember what's in it. I think I tried to read it once, but it was, I'm sorry to say, boring. I still have it. You can borrow it if you like."

She rises, goes to the rolltop desk that once belonged to Grandpa, removes a thin black file, and hands it to me.

A ghostly record; typeface and typing paper from long ago; letters with faded contours. Perhaps the typist who transcribed Grandpa's handwritten original—for I imagine that's what happened—struck the keys with inconsistent force, or perhaps the grommet that engaged the inking ribbon was loose and the machine in need of service, for some letters are firm and robust, others so fragile and spidery they seem about to float off the brittle pages.

What do I do with it? What would a historian do?

I draw a chart with dates and geographical place names, order a tome on South African history from Amazon, request books and articles from my university's interlibrary loan service, and read into the night until, exhausted, I fall asleep. Places, men, and events drift off Grandpa's "memoranda" into my dreams: 1896 his birth in Esirany, Russia; 1906 he, his mother, and his brother join his father in London; in 1912, fleeing poverty, he migrates to South Africa; tersely, he notes the 1913 General Strike; in more detail, the 1914 South African Rebellion of British-hating Boers; and, in more detail, enlisting with the Transvaal Scottish to take South West Africa from the Germans—a campaign in which, he notes, General Beyers drowned in the Vaal River.

Though he spent his first ten years in Russia, there's no mention of life there. He begins his story in England:

I began to hate the country for no other reason than that the poverty was too much for me. So, all my spare time I used to spend at the Docks trying to get away from my present surroundings. At last in 1912 I managed to migrate to South Africa. We travelled steerage, which is the lowest class, like a lot of cattle, restricted to a very small area. The hold had no ventilation and crossing the Bay of Biscayne in the winter was like hell. The place smelled of piss and urine.

Really, Gramps? "*. . . for no other reason*"? Surely there were other reasons: Anger at your father, a barrowman barely able to support his family by delivering timber to cabinetmakers and spending whatever free time he had in shul wrapped in his tallit, praying? Anger at your mother, who struck you so hard on the side of your head that you forever bore the scar—a three-inch white line behind your left ear? Is it not said that an exile is the son of a father whose presence does not detain him; and, likewise, that the exile is a stranger to his mother whom he does not call and from whom he asks nothing?

When World War I broke out Grandpa enlisted with the Second Transvaal Scottish:

We were then sent to Walvis Bay, the nearest spot to German South West Africa. Swakopmund and Walvis Bay were desert land. The sand dunes were knee deep and forever shifting and it was all very dry and there were no jetties and the troops had to be taken off in lighters and it took Generals Botha and Smuts and their associates three months to get the men and equipment for us and for Luderitz and the mounted men and there were no women at all, so they arranged concerts and boxing bouts at night and other sports during the day, and it was my lot to be selected to fight L. Townes, the Cape Province lightweight champion, as I was about the weight. It was supposed to be a six round contest, but it only lasted three rounds because the Commanding Officer stopped the fight as it became too rough, but my prestige and reputation left a special significance with the officers and men and the Second Scottish were very proud of me.

I wish I could tell Grandpa that I too am writing a memoir and that it grieves me that I never asked him about his content or his process; that I have so many—too many—questions:

Were you afraid, Gramps, when you set out?

Were you lonely?

> We captured Moschi, Kilimanjaro, Aruscha, Kumbuluim and Pienaars Heights, but we got stuck in Kondoa Irangi and then the rainy season started. Most of us went down with malaria, and we had no more stamina and could go on no further. Many men and officers died from malaria, black-water, dysentery, beri-beri, from bites and stings from scorpions, spiders, snakes, tse-tse flies, mosquitoes, jigger fleas, wasps, wild bee stings and lice. We were starving. I saw men get sunstroke and go mad. Most of the men were lousy and green from being doped with quinine, which is bitter as gall. We looked like Napoleon's Army after the retreat from Moscow in 1812. What a sorrowful plight. The horses too were tired and developed some kind of sickness. Their mouths used to go frothy and we were obliged to shoot them because wild dogs and vultures would devour them while alive.
>
> After serving approximately two hundred and thirty days, on the 9th of November, 1917 I was discharged with a certificate saying that I was permanently unfit for tropical service. I had malignant malaria.

I remember Grandpa as inarticulate, but now, reading and rereading, I think I was wrong, for I discover language skills I never knew he had. Moreover, there's an energy, a vitality to the writing that allows me to experience a physical being different from the frail emphysematous old man I called Grandpa or, sometimes, Gramps.

Although declared "unfit for tropical service," Grandpa was not done with adventuring. He became a rough-riding cowboy in a Schlesinger film; a mine laborer; a stevedore; a cook in a sailing vessel—a canvas-rigged ship with an all-Scandinavian crew that sailed to Angola and Montevideo and the Sargasso Sea and Copenhagen with a crew of sailmaker, carpenter, cook and cook's assistant (Grandpa), sixteen sailors, and two scientists in search of marine life, sailing, oftentimes, through weather so rough that two men were strapped to the big steering wheel that managed the rudder so they wouldn't be washed overboard. At last, in October 1919, having *had enough of the sea for the time being, fit as a fiddle and full of energy*, he returned to the East End in search of his family and saw that all the Jewish shops were closed because, someone explained, it was Succoth, the Festival of Booths. His mother fainted at learning that the man before her was the boy who'd left seven years before; his father, notified in shul that his long-lost son had returned, finished his prayers and came home to greet him. Others, as he notes, came too, for *news travels very fast and very many old and young girls started paying social visits to my parents and so the net was cast and my mother was the biggest culprit and I started taking out a regular girlfriend who after nine months became my wife.*

Wedding photograph of my maternal grandparents Sydney and Rochel/Rachel.

The story shifts:

For me it was the end of the road as a wanderer, and a new road commenced, a very long road. My first move was that I started looking for a business and behold, I purchased a fish and chips shop. It was the roughest, most discordant and most brutal district in London, the Borough of St. Georges, Bermondsey, full of doss houses, vice and immorality. The men's national attire was a cap with a choker around their necks, whilst the women's headgear was a man's cap reversed with its peak at the back of the head, with a long pin to act as a stiletto or dagger in case of emergency.

Though Grandpa's story lacks a narrative arc, he writes great scenes:

In that part of London there was never a night without a fight. The basements under the shops were all infested with large water rats, each basement was a rat warren, added to this were the railway and cheap food shops, and it was very near the River Thames. But nothing compared with some of the human rats. I had to engage an Army strong man as a chucker-out and fortunately he knew most of the roughs by sight. One night a man and woman walked into the shop. As soon as he saw them he whispered: "Gov, you will have plenty of trouble tonight. This man who is known as 'Casty Cannon' is the terror of the district."

Casty Cannon and his woman friend took a table and ordered steak and chips, which was then two and sixpence per person. Then two other women and men joined his party and they too ordered steak and chips. My man Bob served them but they would not pay him, so I came up and said: "Twelve shillings and sixpence please." Casty Cannon said he had never yet paid a dirty Jew. All I could see was red and I swung a terrific right hand blow on his chin and followed it with a few others. I had him at my mercy. Before he could retaliate, during the melee a marble table and most of the food was scattered on the floor, but I shouted to Bob to close the door. I wouldn't let them out unless they paid for the food, and very reluctantly they paid. To my very great astonishment this gang visited my shop again, but on the most amicable terms. It was apparent they carried no animosities. Believe it or not, we actually became friends and if there was any trouble in the shop, Casty would settle it for me.

And then, without giving an explanation, he sells the fish and chips shop and, with his new bride, in 1921 sails back to South Africa—far away from his mother, from his family, and London, though he remained forever linked to the seat of Empire and even to his mother, whom he supported financially until her death decades later. He was, then, twenty-five, determined to become wealthy.

Addressing the intended reader—my preteen younger brother—he notes, with modesty mixed with pride, *This memoranda may not appeal to you as great literature, but I am sure that it will make good reading, this story of a mere boy of a very poor family, to success and riches. I maintain that anyone determined to pursue success, the formula is: great drive, courage and perseverance, which goes a long way towards the stability and security for one's family which is so meaningful.*

Grandpa started Durban Clothing Manufacturers, the factory that became my father's, with a secondhand sewing machine. One machine multiplied into many as he rode the wave of South Africa's expanding economy: industry needed workers; workers needed uniforms; Grandpa made them. With no brand name, style, or gender focus, Grandpa adapted his production to whatever orders came in. In 1936 he got his big break: a lucrative contract to make uniforms for gold mine workers. He became rich.

And he became a collector—paintings, clocks, antique furniture, Persian rugs, and books. He, not Granny, was the homemaker, carefully selecting each item that entered their lovely Cape Dutch house, a five-minute walk from our house. Grandpa regarded each selection as a treasure, though most, I suspect, weren't worth whatever he'd paid—with one exception: Vermeer's *The Glass of Wine. That* was priceless, its worth beyond the reach of money.

I was ten years old when Grandpa brought it home, and I was there when it arrived. Grandpa told me, when I came to his house that morning, that he'd be back soon with something special, and I should wait. And, so, I sat in the kitchen with Granny and drank tea.

Granny was still in her housecoat, not yet strapped into her corset, her soft, white flesh cascading in ripples beneath her robe's thin fabric, her bunions at ease in slippers. A sugar cube behind her dentures, she slurped milky tea from a saucer and dunked stale mandelbrot into her teacup to render it soft enough to dissolve in her mouth. I too drank tea. Though I longed to try Granny's saucer approach, I drank mine from a mug because Granny's habit, when Grandpa caught her at it, made him curse in Yiddish about stupid Russian peasants who couldn't rise above their origins. Granny, hearing him—as he'd meant her to—would shrug, wink at me, giggle, pour another glug into her saucer, lean forward, and, with eyes closed to enhance her pleasure, slurp it down.

I was on my second mug when I heard Grandpa's car drive up to the house. Granny and I rushed to the front door to see what he'd brought home.

Johannes carried a large flat box from the Buick up the steps to the front door. Grandpa, huffing to keep pace with the long-limbed driver, exclaimed, "Be careful. Watch out. Don't drop it. Whoa!" Carefully, Johannes set the box on the black-and-white tiled floor. Grandpa, still breathing heavily from the ordeal of the steps, placed his gray fedora on the hall table beside his treasured big gold clock, removed his jacket—after turning it inside out, as he always did—put it on a dark wooden chair, and bent to open the box, his suspenders stretching across the arc of his white-shirted back. But he was stiff and couldn't reach, and so Johannes bent to help.

"Be careful," Grandpa said, as though he hadn't given warnings enough.

Dropping easily to his knees, Johannes pried the box open and, with Grandpa hovering and issuing more instructions, removed wrappings of tissue paper. Within lay a painting in a large gold frame. Grandpa gestured to a wall, and Johannes propped it there. Granny and I moved closer, Grandpa too, though the painting was too low for him to see without, as I did, dropping to the floor for a good look.

"Well," said Grandpa, "what do you think? It's a rare find. It's by Johannes Vermeer. He's very famous."

Mesmerized by the painting, I almost didn't hear him. Then, aware he'd asked a question and was awaiting my response, I said, "Oh, Gramps, it's the most beautiful of all your paintings."

Grandpa softened, glad of my approval, as though my ten-year-old verdict of an artist I'd never heard of mattered. In those days I had as little art knowledge and vocabulary as Grandpa, but where I was innocent of my insufficiency, Grandpa's troubled him. He was tortured by feelings of inadequacy in all matters cultural, embarrassed he'd had no schooling beyond his bar mitzvah. Art collecting—a visible manifestation of cultural capital—was his way of making up for that.

The Vermeer stayed on the floor propped against the wall for several days, awaiting its permanent placement. Grandpa knew exactly where he wanted to hang it: opposite the front door to the right of the gilded rococo clock that sat under a glass dome on a marble-topped table. Grandpa adored that clock and made sure it was the first thing entering visitors saw; and now he had something equally splendid to arrest their gaze and elicit their admiration. But there was already a painting to the right of the clock, and Grandpa had to figure out where to rehang it so the space could showcase the Vermeer.

The problem was that Grandpa had purchased so many paintings from Jacobs the auctioneer and Simkowitz the antique dealer that there was almost no empty wall space. I don't remember anything about the painting he had to relocate to make room for the Vermeer except that it, like all the others he'd purchased, was dark, gloomy, and difficult to figure out. Until he bought the Vermeer, Grandpa seemed to favor brownish landscapes with toiling peasants, or pictures of bulls and cows resting in dappled shade, though a few—easier to read because pale faces stood out against dark ground—were portraits of sorrowing men and women from long ago.

Grandpa's house was filled with treasures: Persian rugs, some dully brown, others with silky thread that caught the light. There were so many rugs in the formal sitting room that they overlapped, making the surface uneven so that walking there, on special occasions like Passover or Rosh Hashanah when we were allowed into that room, felt like passing over soft earth. And the furniture! Mahogany and dark oak tables, brown leather club chairs with brass studs, and Queen Anne chairs with legs bandier than Granny's. And clocks—lots of clocks that needed keys to wind the mechanism.

Grandpa wound them on Sunday evenings when my aunt's and my family gathered there for early supper. After supper, before his poker pals arrived, my cousin and I would follow him from clock to clock, watching him select the appropriate key from the heavy bracelet-sized key ring encircling his upraised forearm. I never asked if I might wind one, though I always wanted to, and he never offered to let me. Winding the mechanisms was his ritual and pleasure, and it never occurred to him to share it, but I knew he liked having us follow him, watching him open the glass door that covered a face, as though saying *hello*, searching for the right key, inserting it, and then instructing us not to speak while he counted the requisite number of revolutions. Sometimes he'd rotate the hands until the clock chimed and then turn to see if we had also delighted in the sound. Though he strove to synchronize them, they never bent to his will, preferring their own discordant cacophony. At some point he seemed to resign himself to their noncompliance, as though finding comfort in hearing individual voices sequentially announce the final curtain call of a vanishing hour and the possibilities of the one about to begin.

The clocks I remember most vividly are the grandfather clock with its moon-dial face that stood in one corner of the entrance hall, the grandmother clock in the opposite corner, and the three-foot-high, ornate rococo gilt confection under a glass dome on the marble-topped table opposite the front door, its simpering cherubs offering gilded bums and coy smiles in provocative welcome. My mother inherited that clock—her favorite and my least. It traveled to Israel with my parents, then to La Jolla, California, to England, back to California, and now it's back in England in my mother's tiny apartment in a retirement home, its glass dome miraculously intact. Grandpa used to lift the dome to wind the mechanism—a feat of breathtaking delicacy and strength that my parents never attempted, so that time, according to the filigreed hands on the clock's small face, has remained forever fixed at its point of exhaustion after Grandpa last wound it.

Now, more than fifty years later, I wish I'd asked Grandpa about the artifacts he collected, wish I'd walked with him through the house and asked, "Why, Gramps, did you buy this? Why that?" Perhaps I didn't ask because I knew that Grandpa could not have answered. He was not an articulate man, his reticence a defense against exposing his lack of education. Surrounding himself with art was his only way to lay claim to cultural capital, and he could only do so silently, trusting that his beloved treasures would speak for him.

Grandpa couldn't have answered my questions but I, who have spent my life accruing cultural capital, will hazard an answer on his behalf:

Grandpa's mania for collecting followed a period beginning in the middle years of the nineteenth century when ghetto doors opened and Jews seeking opportunity and integration into host cultures began to emulate the cultural practices of educated gentiles: attending theater, symphony, and opera—and collecting art. Art, particularly if it included the human face or form—forbidden in the Torah lest likeness lead to idolatry—was one way to assert secular humanist enlightenment, or, at the very least, claim distance from strict Jewish observance in favor of a different kind of sanctity: the aesthetic.

Grandpa could not have explained this, but I think he felt it. Though deeply rooted in Jewish culture—ill at ease with gentiles, more comfortable with Yiddish than English—he scorned the strict Orthodox observance of his parents, blaming his family's poverty on his father, who spent more time praying than earning money and who, when at home, dutifully followed the precept to be fruitful and multiply, siring one unaffordable child after another on his long-suffering wife.

The paintings Grandpa bought—rich in chiaroscuro, heavy with impasto, veiled in sfumato mystery—declaimed old master credentials, linking him to illustrious collectors like the Rothschilds who amassed old master greats and focused on the Flemish and Dutch schools—perhaps because seventeenth-century Holland was hospitable to Jews fleeing the Inquisition, perhaps because Rembrandt painted Jews with great sympathy. Grandpa didn't belong in the lofty league of Rothschild, but the cultural ethos for moneyed Jewish men of his generation was to follow the Rothschild path, celebrating, as they did, the abundance and availability of beautiful, valuable, and secular objects that proclaimed their owner's affluence and taste.

I wish I'd made an inventory of the objects Grandpa collected, wish I'd photographed every clock and painting. But that was long before I knew the word *inventory*, long before I'd undertake scholarship about collectors and collecting, long before Walter Benjamin's exquisite essay on the passion of the collector, "Unpacking My Library," would become a key text in the seminar on collecting I would teach every semester. Nor, at ten, did I wonder why an uneducated old Jewish man would want to fill his house with objects that spoke more of European civilization than of the shtetl. But at some point I *would* wonder and would regret not having wondered sooner. Additionally, as I ventured more deeply into the discipline of art history, I would wonder why so many names in its pantheon—dealers, collectors, and art historians—were Jewish: Berenson, Duveen, Durand-Ruel, Kahnweiler, Gimpel, Wildenstein, Panofsky,

Guggenheim, Rosenberg, Rosenblum, Castelli, Schapiro, Steinberg, Greenberg, Fried, Krauss, and so forth. And I would realize what I had not known when I took my first art history course: I had entered a profession that *seemed* gentile but was marked and shaped by Jews.

Many of its luminaries had entered the field of art history because other fields, especially in Germany, had not been available to them, and many, like Irwin Panofsky, had focused on Christian art as a path to assimilation, a path away from Jewish identity into a world once off-limits to Jews. Over the years, as I came to understand how much my profession was shaped by Jewish scholars, I began to ponder if I'd been drawn to it because I wanted to affiliate with other Jews negotiating their Jewish identity in a secular world. And then I found myself working backward—from the assimilationist ethos of art history to an engagement with my Jewish identity. Indeed, shortly after I wrote this section, I came across Eunice Lipton's essay "The Pastry Shop and the Angel of Death" in *People of the Book: Thirty Scholars Reflect on Their Jewish Identity*. There, more eloquently than I can, Lipton explains why she became an art historian. I love her explanation so much that I'll present it as true for me, though I read it only recently and it's not, strictly speaking, part of my own autobiography but, rather, an insight I've adopted retrospectively.

> I wanted two things at once when I became an art historian. I wanted to be where Jews were—that is, I wanted a profession that would allow me tacitly to acknowledge my Jewishness through the company I kept—but I also wanted to hide, to be gentile. I wanted to assimilate.... I don't think I ever fooled anyone but myself.

But then, standing with Grandpa, mesmerized, all I knew for sure was that the Vermeer was the most beautiful painting I had ever seen.

Here were blues, greens, oranges, and whites. Cool sunshine and warm pleasure. A man and a woman at a table enjoying themselves. The lady, her glass drained, holds a light-catching goblet over her nose to inhale the lingering fragrance. The man, half smiling, observing her pleasure, waits to deliver more—his hand on the bright white jug, his forearm suspended over the table, his muscles flexed. He's all attention, anticipating the instant she'll take the glass from her face so he can raise the jug, pour, and watch her drink again.

Jan Vermeer: The Glass of Wine, 1658/60
Gemaldegalerie, State Museum of Berlin

It didn't seem dramatic, and yet it was. I couldn't figure out where the drama lay, and I couldn't stop trying to. The painting was a magnet, and I *had* to stand before it every time I visited.

Over the years, Grandpa and I developed a special bond over that painting. At almost every visit we'd stand together and look at it silently. When we were done looking, we'd turn to each other, and Grandpa, always awkward with physical affection, would pat me on the back and say, "You're a good girl."

The Vermeer mattered more to us than to anyone else in the

family. I didn't understand why we loved it so much, but I wanted to; and so, long before the time came for me to go to university, I knew I'd study art history to find out why we loved the Vermeer.

The University of Natal in Durban had no art history program, and so I went away to Johannesburg to study at the University of the Witwatersrand (Wits).

The most important and famous professor in the Department of Fine Arts at Wits was Dr. Martienssen—the university's first woman professor who, in addition to that distinction, had shaped the Department of Fine Arts into the best in the country. People spoke of her vitality, erudition, and brilliance and told me how lucky I was to have an opportunity to study with her, for it was rumored she would soon retire. Though I wasn't, then, familiar with all her scholarship, she seemed to me the living embodiment of the classical world whose art and architecture she knew and loved, for she wore her cropped gray hair in the Caesar style of the Prima Porta Emperor Augustus and, on her body, a floor-length robe with a muted trim about the neck that made her look like a Doric column. At the start of each class as she stood at the lectern gathering her thoughts, I was struck afresh by her appearance and wondered if all great scholars tended to acquire the characteristics of the objects or periods they had dedicated their lives to studying.

A few weeks into my very first art history course, Dr. Martienssen delivered a lecture on the northern Baroque. A jolt went through me, for there on the screen was Grandpa's Vermeer! At last I would learn everything I'd longed to know about the painting. I could hardly wait to hear her words of wisdom.

Dr. Martienssen turned to the screen, then paused, as she often did when a new image took the place of one she'd just shown, to *look*, really *look*, as though she'd never before seen the work. But then, as often happened, she seemed to lose herself in thought. We sat silently, fifty or so undergraduates, waiting for her pondering to run its course and her focus to return to us. I could scarcely breathe, so impatient was I for her revelation. Surely she would explain why the Vermeer so enthralled her, and then I would finally understand why it so enthralled Grandpa and me.

Moments passed. Dr. Martienssen, still and statuesque, seemed as oblivious to the awkward fidgeting in the room as a Doric column to a buffeting Aeolian wind. At long last, with a deep sigh, she turned from the screen, looked toward the projectionist, and said, "Next please," and Grandpa's Vermeer vanished! Tears of disappointment blurred my vision. Panic gripped me. What if Dr. Martienssen retired without sharing her profound insights about Grandpa's Vermeer? Though I'd never before approached her, I resolved, as soon as class was over, to tell her I'd grown up with *The Glass of Wine*.

She finished early, as she often did, as though to convey that whatever she'd imparted was enough, more than enough, and we could use the remaining time to linger in the auditorium to let the echo of her words and the fading auras of the images sink in. Mustering my courage, I went down to the lectern where she was gathering her papers, which I always wondered why she brought, for she never glanced at them, though she treated them tenderly, as artifacts precious and fragile.

I stood beside her waiting for what felt like the longest time. She seemed unaware of my presence. I was about to give up when she turned to me, fixing on me the kindest gray eyes, seeming surprised to find a student at her side.

"My grandfather owns the Vermeer you showed. I grew up with it."

She frowned, lowering her head to peer at me over the tops of her glasses, but something took the frown from her face and her eyes again grew kind.

"The original," she said, "hangs in the Gemaldegalerie in Berlin. It's been there since 1901. Perhaps your grandfather owns a copy or a print?"

"Oh, I thought Grandpa's was the original. He bought it at

auction, and he always told me it was precious."

"It is," she said, "and you are fortunate to have a grandfather who brings such a treasured image home for his grandchildren to see and love. The only reason to collect an object is if you love it so much you can't bear not to see it every day. Your grandfather has good instincts and, I suspect, has created a home with many treasures for you to love."

Right then I didn't care that Grandpa's Vermeer was a print. I loved it too much to care for such a detail. What I wanted to know was what made Grandpa and me love it so much.

"I was hoping," I said, "that you could explain what makes the painting so special, why Grandpa and I—and you too—can't stop looking at it."

Dr. Martienssen took a deep breath and then smiled—a huge smile that filled the dimmed auditorium with light.

"What really matters," she said, "is that you and your grandfather have been *affected* by the image, that you opened yourself to what I can only describe as its *mysterious humanity*. That is the quality that makes us love art. Art history can't teach that. You have to *feel* it, *apprehend* it—the way you and your grandpa do. Art history can get in the way of that because it crowds your mind with facts and history. If you become an art historian, if this becomes your profession, remember always to *look* and *feel*, to be open as you and your grandfather are to the mysterious humanity of great art."

When I returned to Durban after my first term at university, I visited my grandparents. They had, by then, moved from their Cape Dutch house on Musgrave Road to a high-rise apartment on the beachfront. Now Grandpa could look every day at the Indian Ocean that had brought him to South Africa so long ago, inhale the sea air that had filled his nostrils with the fragrance of distant places when, as a boy, he'd hung out at the London Docks and wondered what lay beyond.

We went directly to the Vermeer, which now hung in the dining room, opposite the chair where Grandpa sat for breakfast, lunch, and dinner.

"Well," said Grandpa, struggling against the emphysema that would, in two years, put him in a hospital bed where he would die, away from his home and treasures.

"Well, what do you think? You're an art maven now. You can tell me all about it."

"I think," I said, "that I'm fortunate to have a grandfather who brings home beautiful objects for his grandchildren to see and love—especially this one. I missed your Vermeer, Gramps. I could hardly wait to come home and see you both and stand with you in front of the painting."

He patted me.

"You're a good girl," he said, "a very good girl."

We looked a while longer, and I thought about Dr. Martienssen and what she'd said about *mysterious humanity*. Grandpa patted me again.

"I need to lie down," he said. "You're a good girl," he repeated. "A tonic."

Experiencing Vermeer wasn't the only lesson I learned from Grandpa. As I grew older, I discovered other lessons in his "office"—a large upstairs room at the farthest end of the house, its heavy damask curtains always drawn. Against one wall was the massive rolltop desk my mother now owns; opposite was a large oak bookcase with leaded glass-paned doors, each with a tiny key. Sometimes Grandpa took us there and showed us precious things he'd locked away in the safe: gold coins, gold watches, diamond and ruby brooches he'd bought for Granny that she wore only on High Holy Days or when my brothers had their bar mitzvahs or, in 1932, when Jascha Heifetz, a fellow Litvak, played in Durban's City Hall and the city's Jewish community packed the venue. The office was Grandpa's private sanctuary, the only room in the house whose door was always closed and, I assumed, locked.

Once, when I was twelve and Grandpa was playing chess in the family room with Old Man Goldberg—the two of them exclaiming, swearing, and cursing in Yiddish as their battles on the board grew fiercer, and Granny was in the kitchen, preparing endless cups of milky tea to soothe their throats and spirits—I went upstairs with my library book. I passed Granny's bedroom, then Grandpa's, Grandpa's bathroom, then Granny's, then two guest bedrooms, to the end of the hall to the closed door of Grandpa's office and tried the handle. It yielded, and I went directly to the bookcase and unlocked every door.

The woody scent of old leather prickled my nose as I gazed at rows of embossed bound sets with gold-lettered titles I couldn't recall having seen Grandpa read. Beneath was an edition of the *Encyclopedia Britannica* much older than ours. What lay below? I kneeled to check, for the lower contents seemed brighter and more contemporary. There, almost hidden, lay dozens of copies of *True Detective,* their spines frayed and creased from having been folded, front cover to back cover, as though Grandpa had settled into a comfortable chair and read each from start to finish.

On every cover was the drawing of a beautiful woman—wasp-waisted, red-lipped, bare-necked in a low-cut dress, some in a state of dishabille. A few covers included men in the background—in raincoats with hats pulled low on their brows or hiding conspicuously behind a bush. Others showed a man's hand covering the woman's mouth, or two hands around her neck, her mouth in a silent scream. Headlines in capital letters told the reader of "California's Terrifying Crime of Passion: Girl in the Trunk," "Strange Fate of Arizona Heiress," "The Riddle of Oregon's Dismembered Brunette," and "Tacoma, Washington: I Buried Her Alive."

Jammed into the far left of the shelf were two thick books, one the color of tobacco, the other red. Their titles: *The Kinsey Report:*

Sexual Behavior in the Human Female and *The Kinsey Report: Sexual Behavior in the Human Male.* Cross-legged on the floor, I began to read, hoping that Grandpa and Old Man Goldberg were fired up enough for several more battles and that Granny would offer Old Man Goldberg the cold fried fish she always saved for him because he'd told her no one made it better and he had no one at home to cook for him, and because he was, I once heard Grandpa tell Granny, poor, and it was a mitzvah to feed him. Then I'd have time to explore Grandpa's library.

Under an atlas beneath the shelf of *True Detective*, I saw a different stack of magazines. I pulled out the top one: *Gala Holiday Issue, Playboy, Entertainment for Men, January 1962.* A man dressed in a red tuxedo with a white rabbit's head and long, pointy ears sat on a red sofa holding a red drink in a red martini glass. On the wall behind him were four pictures framed in gold of girls—naked, or almost naked, except for tops so sheer they might just as well not have worn anything at all. One had fluffy pompoms on her high-heeled slippers.

I wanted to read and read, but I could hear Grandpa and Old Man Goldberg talking—a different sound from when they played chess—and so I knew that Old Man Goldberg would soon leave and that Grandpa would wonder what I'd been up to, so I put the magazines and the two Kinsey books back where they belonged, picked up my own book, closed the bookcase doors and Grandpa's office door, and went downstairs.

"What have you been up to?" Grandpa asked.

"Reading," I said, holding out *Jude the Obscure*.

"You're a good girl." He patted me on the back, and then we went to stand before the Vermeer as we always did. For the first time I noticed that the lady drinking wine had a flat chest—not at all like the ladies on the *Playboy* cover. I brought my right hand to my left shoulder and pressed my forearm against my chest. It, too, was flat. I wondered if it would stay flat like Vermeer's lady or grow round and full like the *Playboy* girls and if my waist would ever be as narrow as the waists of the beautiful women on the covers of *True Detective*.

But then, looking at Vermeer's painting, I registered something else I'd never noticed: between the man and the woman was a tension that somehow connected Vermeer to *True Detective* and *Playboy*. I didn't, then, have the language or experience to articulate what that tension was, but I do now: the erotic, which undergirds all powerful representations.

I remember when Grandpa lay dying in hospital and I came from Jo'burg to Durban to see him and he was so weak he could hardly speak, but he asked how long I'd be home, and my mother said, "'Til Tuesday," and I said, "I think I'll stay 'til Wednesday," and he patted my hand and said, "I hope it's 'til Wednesday. You're a tonic." When it was time to go, I didn't bend to kiss him because I was afraid of disturbing the tubes that disappeared into his veins and his nose, and he said, "It's not contagious, you know. It's nothing you can catch," and then I bent; but right then the nurse came in and said, "You've tired him. And please don't touch the tubes," so I never kissed him goodbye, and I never saw him again.

PORTRAIT #3: MY FATHER: MAN ABOUT TOWN

Grandpa Sydney and my father had different perspectives on England, Africa, and Empire.

Grandpa spent his teen years in London, when Britian was at the height of her global hegemony. He would have been exposed to the national ethos that Britannia ruled the waves and to the romance of imperialism's terra incognita. Though he hated much about Britain, he fought for her in World War I and never questioned Britain's colonialist imperialism, nor his imbrication within it.

In contrast, my father, more educated, more psychologically nuanced, passionately interested in history and biography, was conflicted about being a white man in Africa. He was restless, unhomed, caught between the seductions and guilt of white privilege, convinced that apocalypse was inevitable and that he had to get us out before it came—but only after he'd made money so he could support us elsewhere in the manner we'd grown accustomed to in South Africa.

Where Grandpa looked *away* from the imperial centers, my father looked *toward* them, to London, Paris, Rome, and New York—glamorous, urbane, sophisticated, culturally rich, the pulsing hearts from which great men like Caesar, Napoleon, Disraeli, Churchill, and Roosevelt directed the course of history. As a boy living in a small dorp in the Western Cape in remote southern Africa, he felt the centers of empire beckon. Surely, if he could get there, he'd shed his provincialism and come into his own? Surely, *there* power could hold apocalypse at bay...

In my mind's eye I see my father wobbling on a ledge trying to figure out if he should hold on a little longer or leap off. He was a man for whom leaping off precluded return and who struggled to repress the agonies of second thought—about his business practices, his personal relationships, and his religion. But the unconscious scorns closed doors; in his late nineties my father was tormented by dreams that awakened him in the loneliest hours of the night, sending him tottering with his walker down the hall outside his and my mother's apartment as if, beyond his bedroom, he might escape the specters that had entered his dreams until, exhausted, he'd return home to a chair to wait for dawn or, if he were lucky, to fitful dozing.

He was uncomfortable in his skin, the psoriasis that plagued him all his life a too-literal manifestation of his chronic unease, his uncertainty of where he belonged, of where and how to position himself. Fluent in Yiddish, the language his parents spoke at home, he delighted in chance encounters with Yiddish speakers as accomplished and articulate in the language as he. Active in Durban's Jewish community, he helped raise funds for a Jewish golf club because no club in Durban would admit Jews, and he and my mother wanted to play. Further, he was a major fundraiser for a Jewish day school, for he wanted my brothers to study Hebrew and Jewish culture, to be with other Jewish children, and to be spared the anti-Semitism my sister and I endured at our Anglican girls' school. And when he finally moved his family out of South Africa, he moved them to Israel.

And yet he railed with near-fanatical zealotry against Judaism, making enemies by denouncing Jewish observance and taking pleasure in the discomfort his tirades triggered. With relish he often repeated a story about an impoverished, pious Jew who came to his clothing factory to request a free suit and stipulated no *shatnez*—cloth containing both wool and linen—because the Leviticus code of holiness prohibits such mixing; my father shouted the man out of the factory. And a San Diego friend of his who was also a friend of mine told me he invited my father to a Shabbat service—which my father attended, though he pointedly turned his back on the Torah, the most sacred text in Jewish culture, when it was taken out of the ark. I wondered if my father had viewed the invitation as an opportunity to express his scorn for the Torah, or to alienate his friend and the congregants, or if he felt the need to test the God he purported not to believe in, or if he were testing himself to see how far he would go—or all of the above.

In his early eighties he handed me a six-page paper he'd written: "A Plain Man's Search for God." *He* was the "plain man"—a self-designation that, for me, held a mixed message: *I'm a plain man, a small-town boy from the country, yet thoughtful and profound enough to tackle this weighty issue.* In the manuscript he recounted his distress when, as a child, he learned that millions of Chinese had drowned in a flood of the Yangtze Kiang River. He could not understand how a loving God could have allowed that. The same for the Holocaust.

The point to which his plain man's search led him was not God but Spinoza, the great seventeenth-century philosopher deemed a heretic by Amsterdam's Jewish community. The community issued a writ of *cherem*—a form of banning, shunning, ostracism, or excommunication—on Spinoza, calling for him to be cursed "by day . . . when he lies down and . . . by night when he rises up . . . separating him for his injury from all the tribes of Israel with all the curses of the covenant which are written in the Book of the Law." Spinoza was my father's hero.

I think about my father's names, Morris Abraham; in Hebrew, *Moshe Avraham*, the two most revered names in Jewish history—Moses, who led a captive people to freedom and transmitted to them the Ten Commandments as well as the 613 other laws that govern ritually observant Jewish life; and Abraham, the father of monotheism. Was my father burdened by those names? Might he have been happier with a name like his brother Sonny, so much less fraught with the weight of Judaism?

When my father was in his early nineties, I asked him about his names: How was it for him, an atheist, to go through life with the names of Judaism's most revered prophet and most revered patriarch?

He told me he never thought about his names. They were, he said, just his names. It is I, too ruminative, who chews over them, wondering about my father-as-Moses leading his family out of South Africa to other promised lands. Though he gave little thought to his given names, he thought about our family name: Berelowitz. It was, he opined, "too Jewish," "too Lithuanian," and he advised the younger of my two brothers to change his to something more neutral, less Jewishly identifiable.

When my father took over Grandpa's factory in the early 1950s, he developed a radically different vision for its future: not Grandpa's brandless, cut-make-and-trim model geared to the manufacture of industrial uniforms but elegant suits for the upwardly mobile middle class, men like himself yearning to overcome outsider provincial inadequacy. Dreaming of London, Paris, Rome, and New York, he developed a brand name, *Man About Town*, with four slightly different styles: The Look of London, The Look of Rome, The Look of Paris, and The Look of New York. If he couldn't live in one of those centers, he could dress himself and other men as though they did.

I once asked him what inspired the name: Man About Town.

"It just came to me," he said, "and I knew it was right."

Of course it was. Man About Town was my father's dream—one he succeeded in exporting to Britain, for British menswear retailers bought his suits. He made exportability—for himself, his family, and his product—a reality.

In the early years as the company transitioned from Grandpa's to my father's vision, the two men clashed. Similarly hot-tempered, aggressive, and strong-willed, they fought frequently and bitterly. Often my father would return home in a rage because Grandpa had shown up at the factory and interrogated the bookkeeper about orders and debts. Their conflicts affected our family life because they turned into fights between my parents.

In the early years when my father was still struggling to realize his vision for Durban Clothing, he often had to go to Grandpa, cap in hand, to request a loan to make payroll. But his vision prevailed; he made Grandpa, a principal shareholder, much wealthier, and Grandpa came to respect my father. The two men grew to love each other. Grandpa, on his deathbed, gave my father his prized wristwatch and praised him for being a devoted husband and father.

Man About Town is part of my family's history. It is also part of the history of South Africa—even to the extent of making an appearance in the postapartheid literary canon—something I discovered with a shock in January 2014.

I was in a hotel room in Salt Lake City, Utah, with my husband Alan after a day of snowboarding in the glorious Wasatch Mountains. Alan, passionate about motor sports, was reading *Car and Driver*. I was reading Marlene Van Niekerk's weighty novel

Triomf, written in Afrikaans but translated into English. Published in 2005, the novel takes place in 1994 on the eve of the country's first democratic election after the fall of apartheid. It concerns a family of inbred Afrikaners, the Benades, whose extreme endogamy and hermetic isolation is a hyperbolic parody of the Afrikaner ideology of white race blood purity. Overwhelmed by the changes that have swept the country since apartheid's collapse, in mortal fear of the impending general election, the Benades family concocts "The Great North Plan"—they'll flee South Africa in their beat-up car and head north to a country "where you can still live like a white man. With lots of kaffir boys and girls to order around, just as we please." Father Benades reminds his son of his "smart pants" locked away in a steel cabinet with other treasured possessions. The label on the pants, he recalls, is "Man About Town": [When we] "go to the North . . . you're going to have to get back into your smart clothes. Your Man About Towns."

I remember the moment I read that passage with its symbolically laden reference to my father's brand. Suffused with a sudden chill, I dropped the book and looked out the picture window to the snow-clad mountains. *Yes*, I thought, *I am "north," I and everyone else in my family. We have lived my father's Great North Plan.*

Years later, I had another book-generated moment of shock about my father, another acknowledgment of his success and identification with Man About Town.

The year was 2022, more than a year after my father died. Struggling to finish this manuscript, immersed in research about South Africa, I encountered, online, a book that seemed relevant: *Durban: 1824–1974*. What might it show? How might it tug at memory? Though it was expensive, I *had* to order it. When it arrived, I tore open the package and hunkered down at my desk to go through its seven-hundred-page celebration of 150 years of Durban's history. Slowly, I turned the pages, delighting in photographs from long ago, reliving memories. After the pictorial history came essays on Durban's entrepreneurs. Suddenly I screamed. My husband, alarmed, ran to my office.

"Look! My father! Look!"

On page 191: a photograph of *Mr. M. Berelowitz, Chairman*, beside a big photospread of his factory with a large sign, *Man About Town*, emblazoned across the entrance. My father at the height of his powers, nostrils flared; my father as industrialist, as entrepreneur, as founder/genius behind his iconic brand. My father who pushed us all to leave. My father *as* Man About Town.

Durban 1824-1974

Jewish Men Running: Three Portraits   65

3

Reasons to Leave

THREE HISTORIC EVENTS IN THE LATE 1950S AND EARLY 1960S kept my father's focus on leaving South Africa. Those events were close at hand: two occurred on the street in front of our house, another on the street outside my father's factory. The two on our street I witnessed, and though they happened more than sixty years ago, I have never forgotten them.

Cato Manor

My mother and I thought it was hail, the sudden staccato drumming when skies open and hailstones hammer the asphalt. But the sky was a cloudless blue. Then we heard the shouting, in Zulu, men's voices. Through the window of my parents' upstairs bedroom, we saw them: barefoot men running along Musgrave Road, their feet pounding the asphalt, their leader punching the air with his right fist: *Amandla!* Power. The men behind responded: *Amandla, Ngawethu!* Power to us! *Amandla!*

My mother grabbed my arm, pulled me back from the window, and jerked the drapes shut.

"It's dangerous. Don't look. Don't let them see you. Go to your room. Stay there. Find something to read." Obedient, I turned away. Was that the moment when turning away became my default response, a reactive pattern I'm still struggling to overcome?

Decades later, when I asked my mother for her memories of that day, she remembered only the call from my headmistress: "Come at once for your daughters. There is rioting on the streets. Students cannot walk home."

For my mother, the scene of the men has vanished. I don't fault her for that. Events imprint differently for each of us. But for me, although I turned away, the moment was fraught, shattering the placid suburban landscape of my childhood, triggering again the chilling impact of my father's quayside warning. And though it happened decades ago, I still, in my mind's eye, see the men running and shaking their fists at the sky, still hear their voices crying out.

Many years later, when I became obsessed with informing myself about what I had turned from, I learned that the riots began in Cato Manor, a mixed-race township five miles from my home: an all-white neighborhood on the Berea, a sea-breeze-cooled, four-hundred-foot elevated ridge above the lowland mix of Africans and Indians.

Berea homes were spacious, many with pools and tennis courts, on lush green lawns rimmed by pretty flower beds, picture perfect, set back from quiet sidewalks. The children who dwelled there attended private schools; in the afternoons our mothers drove us to swimming, ballet, karate, soccer, and elocution classes; and in the evenings, when our fathers came home, we ate suppers of roast chicken and potatoes followed by desserts of fresh fruit and ice cream—all prepared and served by live-in African servants who'd made our beds after we'd left for school.

In Cato Manor, 160,000 residents—mostly African but also a small remnant of Indians—occupied makeshift shacks of cardboard and iron scraps with inadequate or no sewage or electricity, with no streets or sidewalks. Their ragged barefoot children—largely unschooled and generally malnourished—played among pigs and chickens or languished on iron cots during outbreaks of typhoid.

Five miles is a short distance. A child can walk it. Angry, barefoot men can quicky run it. But from a cultural and political perspective, *those* five miles spanned a gulf between a first and third world.

The government's policy was to widen the physical distance between races while maintaining economic interdependence, and so the white overclass, wholly reliant on Black and brown labor, fearing interracial social relations, legislated separate areas for different races. Accordingly, in the 1950s, the Durban city administration, deciding that Cato Manor was too close to the white city, rezoned it "white." Pursuant with the government's 1950 Group Areas Act, people of color were to be forcibly removed and relocated into zones restricted to their racial identity. Buses would bring them into the white city in the mornings and take them away in the evenings. Removal of Indians to Chatsworth township took place in the early 1950s. The relocation of Africans was scheduled for the late 1950s.

Though Cato Manor houses were pitiful shacks, they were homes, and their occupants would not lightly surrender them.

My father's factory was on Cato Road on the outskirts of Cato Manor. A few years ago, long after the events I'm struggling to piece together, seeking to better understand my father's dire warning to my young self, I asked him what he remembered about the riots. He was, then, ninety. My mother was eighty-two.

They lived, then, in La Jolla, a coastal suburb of San Diego, a twenty-minute drive from where I lived with my husband. They had moved to the United States from Israel in 1984, first to a ranch-style house near the beach and then, twenty years and several residences and one more country later, to this nineteenth-floor apartment in a luxury assisted-living facility.

On the Sunday I set out to question my father, I found him, as usual, in the living room in the wingback chair he'd sat in since forever. The furnishings in the room, like the chair, were constants no matter where my parents had lived since their emigration in 1978, for they had the same treasures, the same household goods they'd had thirty years ago in Durban: two large drawings by Elizabeth Frink, a Dali, a Motherwell, a Frank Auerbach, a Hunderwasser, and a big, 4 x 4 magenta-blue op-art painting by Yvaral that punched the room to attention and proclaimed my mother's distinctive taste, her willingness to mix the contemporary with the traditional.

One reason my parents had purchased art was because my mother loved it. But there was a more important practical reason: Investment-quality art was a way to move hard assets out of South Africa without incurring the suspicion of the South African Securities and Exchange Commission, which by the mid-1970s strictly monitored the transfer of capital out of the country. But art bundled into a citizen's shipment of household goods was hard to intercept. And so my parents bought investment-quality art, enjoyed it while they still lived in Durban, then shipped it out with their furniture and sold most of it to fund their new lives. The few pieces in their apartment were all that remained from what had once been a respectable collection.

My parents were Anglophiles, and my mother's baseline aesthetic, though punctuated with modern flourishes, harkened back to the tasteful clutter of late nineteenth- and early twentieth-century British décor. The brown rug beneath the furniture was Persian, the chairs were antique—Victorian and Edwardian—upholstered in velvety creams. The outer periphery of the room held a couple of small occasional tables whose surfaces were crowded with photographs of my maternal grandparents. They were long deceased by this time, but their presence—in the form of artifacts my mother treasured—filled the room, most notably my grandfather's rolltop desk, his gilded rococo clock, and my grandmother's collection of kiddush cups. There were no photographs of my paternal grandparents. My mother hadn't liked her mother-in-law and my father's father had died before my parents met, so he held no place in her sensibility. She'd relegated her in-laws' photographs to the wall between my father's office and the guest bathroom.

Though I arrived at their apartment shortly before noon, my father was still in his robe, slumped into the embrace of his wingback chair, his eyes closed in weary withdrawal, his mouth downturned, his skin slackly gray, his right fist clenched. A dribble of breakfast cereal had formed a dried crust on his robe; a tea stain discolored the breast pocket that bore the insignia in blue cursive stitching, *Royal Caribbean*. A miasma of staleness hung about him, and I felt a moment's misgiving about opening a door to the past I wasn't sure he'd want to pass through.

I kissed them, made the usual inquiries about how well or poorly each had slept, and then launched into the issue I longed to explore: "Dad, I've been thinking about the Cato Manor riots. Your factory was right there. What do you remember?"

"The riots? Oh Joey, it was a frightening time. And I remember everything."

His eyes opened, he sat straighter and let go the clench of his fist. Remembering seemed to enliven him.

He told me he heard the rioters before he saw them. They sounded, he said, like a stampede of wildebeest—sudden, loud, unstoppable, their momentum seeming to shake the earth. They were shouting in Zulu. Their shouts sounded like a war cry. Then he saw them running along Cato Road wielding pangas, machetes, and knobkerries.

His memories were uncannily close to mine. Had we seen the same cohort of men? I didn't think so because the men running on Musgrave Road had not wielded weapons. I wasn't sure what to make of how similar our recollections were. Had we, long ago, shared impressions of that day so that his memories and mine had somehow melded, each absorbing something from the other, or had we both appropriated newspaper reports and turned them into memories? I didn't think so because I didn't, then, read newspapers.

His eyes widened and his breath came faster.

"You probably don't remember the factory, Joey. There were big windows on the street side. People could see in. It was bloody dangerous. We were vulnerable as all hell. I ordered my Indian workers to lie down under the sewing and cutting tables so they couldn't be seen, and I lay there with them."

In the story he told me, he was a hero, a savior to his Indian workers: He shut the factory and organized his white workers into a convoy to drive the Indians home to their families because buses for Indians weren't safe and cars with Indian drivers were being attacked and burned and their drivers beaten and killed. He, too, drove—a frightening journey through the streets of Cato Manor, where Indian homes, shops, and cars were on fire and the streets were littered with glass and smoldering paraffin tanks.

"The whole township was burning." He shuddered.

I was puzzled. What he described sounded more like the Cato Manor riots of 1949, when African residents of Cato Manor attacked Indians, many of whom were landowners rack-renting shacks to Africans, who were not allowed to own property. In 1949 my father did not have a factory on Cato Road and could not have made the intervention he described to me. Almost nothing I'd read about the 1959–60 riots pointed to Indian–African conflict. For one thing, by the late 1950s few Indians remained in Cato Manor. They'd been relocated to Chatsworth township.

But I'd asked for his memories, and it didn't feel right to dispute them, however much I doubted them.

"And then I drove home," he said, "to check on you lot and take your mother to the Edward Hotel for a drink to get away from it all, from that awful bloody day."

This I took issue with: "You took Mom to the Edward for a *drink*? You left us at home with a nanny when there were riots on our street?" My mother emerged from the kitchen, red nail polish bottle in hand, and sat down on the white sofa.

"We never left you," she said. "*Of course* we never left you. You came with us to the Edward."

"I don't remember taking the children," said my father, irritated she'd contradicted him. "I remember the two of us going, not the children. We never took them to the Edward in the evenings."

"*Of course* we took them. We wouldn't have left them. We had to get as far as possible from Cato Manor."

I believed my father, aligning myself with him, as I always had. Besides, I had no memory of accompanying them and was sure that *had* I gone, I'd remember it, for the Edward was a special place, and I have distinct and clear recollections of the few times I went there.

Built in 1909 on Durban's main coastal strip, the Edward was named for Britain's playboy king, Edward VII. It was Durban's fanciest hotel, grand in the British colonial tradition, with marble floors, crystal chandeliers, potted palms, and whirling ceiling fans. Princes, field marshals, millionaires, and movie stars had stayed there in the glory days of the Empire; and though 1959–60 was the Empire's twilight, the Edward still exuded aristocratic privilege, still held allure, was still a container for desire and fantasy.

My father lived there when he first moved to Durban. Not, of course, in a grand suite, but in the older, cheaper annex that, in the early days, accommodated the valets and butlers of illustrious and wealthy guests. My mother, who saw his room when they were courting, described it years later as *shabby*, her eyes widening in mock shock as she relived her discovery that her handsome suitor, who claimed the prestigious Edward as his address, occupied a substandard, rock-bottom economy room in the annex.

Still, my father took pleasure in having lived there for almost two years. It made him feel sophisticated, less like a bumpkin from a small country town in the boondocks of the Western Cape. He loved the grand lobby and the elegant service of his evening scotch on the rocks and the fancy restaurant, where the head waiter, delighting in the wide-eyed wonder of an appreciative and charming young man, brought him the freshest langoustines, the choicest steaks, and the most buttery slices of smoked salmon—delights otherwise beyond the reach of my father's budget, though in line with his aspirations.

My mother had her own history with the Edward—partying there as a young unmarried woman, dancing to the hotel's big band orchestra into the wee hours of the morning. She was a gifted dancer and knew it, and she broke hearts and exulted in their fracture. Three

My father in his mid-twenties.

of her seven marriage proposals took place at the Edward, numbers she'd recite into her nineties, reminding her children and anyone else who'd listen that she'd once been, as she put it, *sexy*. Even now, when she tells and retells those stories, I picture her suitors watching her spin in and out of another man's arms, tossing her curls to the tempo of the paso doble while they ordered another drink to drown their jealous sorrows.

My mother age nineteen.

For my parents, the Edward resonated with the heady intoxications of youth, before the responsibilities of running a large men's clothing factory or managing a household of three live-in servants and three young children—and, in 1959–60, a fourth on the way. The Edward was their carefree zone of happiness, the place they instinctively went the day riots tore Cato Manor apart and spilled onto our street.

I don't think they took us. But something about the emotional charge of a momentous day so long ago and my parents' quibble about whether they took or left their children opened a what-if for me.

What if they *had* taken us?

My what-if was driven by more than idle fancy. It would have been *normal* for white South Africans to go about their usual lives regardless of a crisis in a township—even if that crisis spilled into a white area—and I was curious to explore what, if any, impact the Cato Manor riots had had on tourists on the main drag of Durban's beachfront. To find out, I turned to archives. My search yielded a single report by a contemporary journalist who remarked on a total disconnect between the events in Cato Manor and the evening's mood on the beachfront: While a township was rocked by government crackdown and mayhem, tourists partied on hotel verandas and drank gin and tonics; their children nagged for Cokes or snow cones or rickshaw rides or, *ag pleez*, another turn on the bumper boats or dodgems until their parents, glasses drained and brains fuzzy with booze, sent them away, out of sight with Black nannies and, thus relieved of the onerous task of parenting, summoned waiters for second—or third—rounds: *Sommer! Lekker! Let's do it!*

What *might* it have been like to accompany my parents to the Edward, to sit with them on the hotel's Art Deco veranda looking out at the spectacle of tourists and watching the sun sink into the Indian Ocean?

I imagine my mother in her favorite blue shirtwaist dress. She's a little thicker at the waist than usual because she's in her second trimester. On her feet are red wedge sandals with ankle straps, the leather matching her red toenails and, of course, her red fingernails. Vicki and I wear party frocks and shiny Mary Janes. Michael has a bow tie clipped into his Peter Pan collar. My father wears slacks and a navy blazer, the top button of his shirt unfastened to signal that his workday is over.

The Edward's Indian maître d' finds us a choice spot with an uninterrupted view of the beachfront. We sit on wicker chairs on the long veranda lined with potted palms, a golden chrysanthemum in a small vase centered on our starched white-clothed table; an overhead ceiling fan enhances the late afternoon breeze that makes Durban evenings so pleasant; an Indian waiter in a white jacket with a red sash from right shoulder to left hip approaches to take our order.

"Good evening, sir, madam." He bows slightly. "What may I bring you and the young ladies and gentleman?"

"What'll you drink, Darling?" my father asks my mother. He almost always calls her Darling unless they're fighting.

"Park Avenue cocktail." She leans forward, her forearms on the white tablecloth, her red-painted fingernails curling around her bare arms. "With four cherries." My mother never says *please* or *thank you* to waitstaff.

"Scotch on the rocks for me," says my dad. "*No* cherries." He says it like it's a joke, and the waiter forces a smile.

"And a Coke for each of the children," my mother adds.

A Coke! This *will* be a day to remember!

The waiter, a silver tray aloft on his upturned, white-gloved hand, returns. Bending at the waist more deeply than the service requires, he places a white cloth napkin in front of each of us, sets down our drinks, and backs respectfully away. My mother hands each of us a cherry, pops one into her own mouth, pulls out the red stem, and lays it on the white napkin. With his finger, my father stirs the ice in his scotch, licks his fingertip, and takes a swig.

We watch the tourists. Easy to spot the out-of-towners. They ride the rickshaws pulled by Zulu men in feathered and beaded headdresses, animal-hair leggings below their knees, bangles of plaited reeds and seeds around their ankles. They're dressed like the Dingaan warriors in my South African history book, who fought the Boers at the Battle of Blood River in 1838 and lost. They have assegais and shields and knobkerries and scary face paint. Some, with passengers in the carriage, suddenly jump up, both legs in the air, tipping the carriage backward as though to eject its occupants who scream in delight and terror; and every now and then a group performs a Zulu war dance: stomping feet, shouting battle songs, and forming into a regiment—the *impi* formation of warriors charging into battle.

I know it's a show, a phony spectacle for tourists. Part of me wants the thrill of the ride, the exhilaration of a tumble from a rickshaw carriage. But mostly I'm glad to be with my parents behind a balustrade on the veranda of the Edward Hotel, drinking a Coke, and not in a rickshaw drawn by a warrior from Dingaan's army.

The sun slips behind the ocean. Cool, salty air drifts onto the veranda. I'm sleepy. The only sound is the hum of ceiling fans. My parents order another drink each. Vicki and I share a second Coke we can't finish. Michael falls asleep on my mother's lap. We watch the twinkly lights on the esplanade, and then we go home to our pretty Tudor house—which I'm not supposed to call home—to pleasant dreams under crisp white sheets freshly laundered by our live-in African domestic servant.

The above was a fantasy, a fictional scene I imagined and then wrote; but now it feels so real that I almost convince myself that we did all go to the Edward, that my mother got it right.

What wasn't make-believe was that government bulldozers razed Cato Manor to rubble.

It became a no-man's-land populated by ghosts.

What caused the rioting?

Apartheid, of course. But what other, more specific issues were there?

My father and I had seen only men running in the streets, but now, digging into archives and articles, I learn that the riots were driven by women. Newspaper headlines proclaimed the events: *The Shebeen Queen Riots* and *The Beerhall Brawl*—acknowledging the presence of women but presenting them as purveyors of drunkenness and antisocial behavior, not as agents capable of instigating unrest. Why did the press identify the riots with women and why were the riots associated with liquor?

As I ruminated, a memory from my childhood surfaced, a memory distant and faded.

I was ten years old, home from school, looking for our cook, Miriam.

"Where is she?" I asked my mother.

"Gone. I fired her. She was brewing *'shimiyana* in her room."

Itisishimiyana: a Zulu word for a drink made from fermented treacle.

"How do you know?"

"Because I've seen men go down the garden path to her room."

"But she has brothers and a boyfriend. Why can't they visit her?"

"She was brewing. I know it. I won't stand for it. And anyway, she's gone, so you'd better get over it."

Let's assume that my mother was correct. Why, my rational adult self asks, would Miriam brew beer on our property?

Because she earned very little and needed money to send to her children, who were restricted by the government to the remote, impoverished native reserves so that she rarely saw them; and because beer brewing, a traditional task of women in Zulu culture, was a way to earn a little extra money.

Of course, the issues are more complicated.

In the 1950s and '60s there were few economic opportunities for African women. Apartheid policy was not gender blind. The government supported the existing traditional subordination of Zulu women by Zulu men, and so it granted housing only to men—bodies necessary for the country's economic growth. This meant that single women in Cato Manor were at risk of being denied housing and being sent back to the native reserves. To entrench themselves within urban life, augment their meager salaries, and support their children, some African women—like Miriam, if my mother was correct—brewed and sold African beer. But the government, wanting to monopolize the lucrative beer market and make urban life more difficult for African women, passed laws that made home brewing illegal. African men could purchase beer only in government-run, male-only beerhalls where the beer had such a low alcohol content that drinkers had to spend more of their earnings to feel its effects.

It was a racket. Beer sales profits funded the meager services the government provided the African community, and the government, wanting to swell its coffers and its sense of its own moral superiority, encouraged drinking in its beerhalls and then pointed to the lax morals of the African men who patronized those halls.

Illegal stills—shebeens—were an alternative. There, men and women could socialize, dance, and consume strong beers with names like *Kill-Me-Quick*, *Skokiaan*, *White Lightning*, *ItsJimiJane*, *Isishimiyana*, and *Darling-What-Have-I-Done*—sometimes laced with methylated spirits or battery acid for an extra kick.

The police, of course, knew about the shebeens, knew that women hid their stills amid Cato Manor's cardboard and paraffin-tin shacks where they and their families slept; and so they raided them, dug up the gallons of brew, poured it onto the dry, dusty earth, hauled the women away to be charged, and then exiled them to remote "homelands" they'd never been to.

Zulu women were angry—not only at the government but at Zulu men for not backing them in their struggles and for limiting them within the African National Congress (ANC), many of whose members believed that women should not be involved in politics. In the 1950s, as their livelihoods and homes came under increasing threat, African women mobilized.

On a Thursday in June 1959, the women gathered.

With the aid of archived photographs and descriptions, I picture them: From early morning they gathered on a sports ground near the big municipal beerhall on the outskirts of Cato Manor. By 10 a.m. there were several hundred. By 11 a.m. they numbered 1,000. By noon 3,000 had gathered. Some came forward to speak.

The leaders tell the crowd they are not traditional women from the native reserve, stupid women who take care of cows and old people, but city women who want a share in the milk and honey, who want housing, civil rights, rights to make their own beer and drink it in their own homes with their menfolk.

Armed with sticks, knives, hatchets, and pieces of firewood, the women run from Cato Manor to the beerhall on Victoria Street in downtown Durban, shouting, "Afrika! Afrika! Our men are boys. We women are the Zulu warriors! Burn the beerhalls, kill the men who drink there!"

It is four o'clock in the afternoon. The beerhall is full of men: stevedores, railroad and factory workers, men whose long shifts began before daybreak, men weary from loading and unloading heavy cargo and from maneuvering dangerous equipment; men too weary even for the social rituals of the shebeen: dancing kwela or jitterbug with the shebeen queen's pretty girls who pressure them to spend more on better-quality *shimeyana*.

Here, in the beerhall, there are no women. Here a man stands in line with his clay pot, his *ukhamba*, from his village. He pays, and the municipal employee fills his canteen with beer. He takes it to a bench and joins brothers from his chief's district and drinks in peace because there are no women. Suddenly there is the noise of women singing and ululating. Where are the police?

Why do the police not drive the women away? The women lift their dresses and show their private parts and the policemen dare not look. Women smash and throw *ukhambas*! Women with sticks, firewood, and knives beat the men, shouting, "You are cowards! You are boys!"

The men shield their faces and heads, but the women beat them. And then a woman lifts her skirt and climbs onto the vat of beer, lowers her buttocks, and empties her bladder into the beer. The women laugh and cheer, "Afrika! Afrika! *Amandla abesifazane*! Women's freedom!"

The men cry: A woman's urine is in our beer! The unclean of woman is in our drink! It is contaminated. We cannot drink it!

The women return to Cato Manor in triumph, but their victory is short-lived. Profits from municipal beer finance subsidized milk to the children of Cato Manor. Because of the women's boycott, beer profits drop and children, already malnourished, receive no milk. For seven weeks the Durban City Council suspends its meager sewerage and water services to Cato Manor. Children die from dysentery, and a typhoid epidemic sweeps through the shacklands. Some women drown themselves in the Mkhumbane River or douse themselves with paraffin and set themselves alight.

The stalwarts resolve to resist to the end.

The end comes.

In January 1960, a police unit composed of seven white and seventeen Zulu policemen enter Cato Manor on a liquor raid. They have information about a shebeen. An informant has told them where to find the shebeen queen's shack and where she has buried her gavine.

I imagine them. The Afrikaners, the white constables: fresh-faced boys from farms in the *platteland* (the rural interior), none older than nineteen, graduates of a six-month training course, followed by six months' service as student constables. Uneducated beyond the equivalent of junior high, their mission is to hold the line, to police, to save white civilization from the forces of barbarism. From the lowest rungs of the white social ladder, they will rise in the police force because they are white.

The African constables are older. They present a problem to the regime, for though they are, from the government's perspective, from the lesser race, their labor and facility with native languages is necessary to help enforce racial laws, especially in the townships. Black policemen are not permitted to give a command to a white policeman, and they are not permitted to apprehend a white suspect. Yet the police force is, for Black constables, a good job, and their work is a channel for upward mobility. Because they are Black, they are not issued guns. Their weapons are sjamboks—leather whips made from the hides of hippos or rhinos—batons, sticks, and sharpened metal poles for flushing "illegals"—those without passbooks, or with passbooks that lack appropriate stamps—and for puncturing liquor stills. Their position is invidious: township Blacks hate and fear them and call them *impimpi* (traitors); white policemen don't trust them, for there is always the risk that a Black policeman will overlook the passbook infringement of a relative, or of a man from his tribe, allowing fealty to his chief to override his commitment to the police force.

It is a lazy, hazy, warm Sunday afternoon. A little too warm, perhaps, for the long sleeves, long pants, and heavy boots of a policeman's uniform. But the men are proud of their uniforms, neatly pressed by girlfriends, mothers, or a Black domestic whose service even an entry-level white recruit can afford. Black Constable Msomi pressed and prepared his own uniform. He is particularly happy with his boots. They are new, with heavy soles and thick leather. Never, as a civilian, could he afford such boots. Last night he polished them with Nugget, rubbing the Nugget into the leather with an old rag and then buffing vigorously with part of a potato sack until they radiated light.

White Constable Joubert lectures the men on their duties for their afternoon shift. Aroused, fired with enthusiasm, they salute and leave the barracks, assigning to the Black constables the task of carrying shovels.

The shebeen queen hears them coming, the sound of nine pairs of boots—beat, beat, beat—on the path to her shack. They do not need a warrant to enter and search. In matters of state security, a warrant is not needed. Illegal brewing is a matter of state security. Illegal residence by a Bantu in an urban area beyond the native reserve is a matter of state security. Barefoot, the woman stands in her box of space on her earthen floor, hands on hips, breasts and belly soft beneath her worn cotton shift, her head wrapped in a *doek*.

"Why you come my house! I nothing here! Nothing! *Humba manje*! Leave now!"

"We will leave after we get the gavine," says Constable Joubert. "We know it is buried under your bed."

"Under my bed only *ebusuku inhlabathi*! Night soil, shit!"

Under her bed, lifted high on bricks so the evil tokoloshe can't reach up and grab her soul while she sleeps, is a pail of viscous yellow-brown liquid. White Constable Joubert tells Black Constable Msomi to remove it so they can search. Removing a Black woman's shit is a job for a Black policeman. Constable Msomi bends to reach the pail. As his hand contacts the rim, three giant cockroaches run out. Startled, he shifts back his weight, and his boot heel closes down on the woman's toes. She screams and demands an apology. Constables Joubert and Biyela immediately apologize on behalf of Constable Msomi. That should do it: two white men apologizing to a Black woman on behalf of a Black man!

But the woman is not appeased. She grabs a bottle and yells, "This is my house, my home! *Voetseck!* Get out! You have no business here."

The policemen retreat. She follows them into the street and throws the bottle at them, yelling, "God will punish. His Kingdom will come. The white man will die. You will be beaten and killed."

A crowd has gathered. Some have pangas. Others grab stones and garbage and throw it at the policemen. Where to turn?

Joubert sees two huts.

"*Vinnig! Binne!* Quick, inside!"

Fleeing into the huts, the policemen barricade themselves. They have twenty-four bullets, but the crowd is eight hundred, mainly women. The women break the doors and windows with rocks and iron bars. The policemen fire. Constable Bekokwake Shandu escapes and contacts his colleagues at a police van.

When at last reinforcements arrive, they find the bodies of nine young policemen: four white, four Black, and Class Sergeant K. Buhlalo. They have been stoned, hacked to death, and disemboweled. Reporters describe the scene as "like an abattoir."

The reinforcement is outraged. They will teach this mob a lesson. This mob will learn what happens when Black women butcher white policemen. First, a baton charge, and then who knows? The commanding sergeant, Van der Merwe, is young. He has never before led a baton charge. He wants it recorded, but there are no police photographers at hand. He spies a reporter: photographer Laurie Bloomfield who works for the *Daily News*.

"Hey! Reporter! We are about to do a baton charge and I want it recorded. What do you need to film it?"

"I will need to stand on the roof of your police van, but first you must reposition it here so I can get a good shot," says Bloomfield.

They reposition the truck. Van der Merwe tells Bloomfield, "We'll issue a third and final warning to disperse. If nothing happens, we'll count down from thirty and then make the charge. Be ready with that camera."

Atop the van, Bloomfield frames his shot: in the light of the setting sun a line of policemen advances on a crowd of women; a penumbra of dust rises as the women dance. Bloomfield's finger is on the shutter. A policeman raises his baton. Bloomfield presses the shutter.

Photographer: Laurie Bloomfield, Cato Manor June 1959.

The photograph appears on every front page of every Argus newspaper and almost every other newspaper on earth that has access to the Associated Press—with one exception—Bloomfield's own paper, Durban's *Daily News*. The editor tells his staff the photograph is too incendiary for immediate publication in a Durban paper.

"It is so strong," he says, "that if we publish it and it gets into Cato Manor tonight, there will be more riots. Let them publish it in Johannesburg and Cape Town."

His discretion was in vain. Thousands of African men took to the streets. And yes, my father was partly correct: There was looting and pillaging of Indian-owned shops. The government dispatched Saracen armored tanks into the township. Police opened fire. People were killed. Shacks were destroyed. Hundreds of people were arrested. Cato Manor's fate was sealed.

I showed my father Bloomfield's photograph.

"Look, Dad. Do you remember seeing this? It wasn't in the Durban papers, but the Jo'burg and Cape Town papers published it. According to the papers, the 1959 and 1960 riots were led by women."

"I've never seen this before," he said. "It's a terrible image. I don't know where you got it. And yes, it shows women. But I'll stick with what I remember: The riot was caused by Indian–African conflict. And now, Joey, I need to take a nap."

I saw no point in arguing. My father had his memories and his convictions—the latter stronger than the former—and I told myself I should respect his resistances. Besides, what was I trying to prove? That he'd known less than he thought he had? That he was paternalistic? That the past frightened him? Or—more likely—was I deflecting my own refusals and ignorance onto my father?

The government, taking no responsibility, sought only revenge. Ten men were sentenced to death by hanging and twenty-one to imprisonment with sentences from one to fifteen years. Government bulldozers flattened Cato Manor, displacing 160,000 people.

A Wind of Change

The third historical event that happened outside my family home took place on Saturday, January 30, 1960, shortly after 2:15 p.m. I know the date and the approximate time not because I remember those details but because the event is part of a documented historical record: the cavalcade of British Prime Minister Harold Macmillan and his wife, Lady Dorothy, en route to the governor-general's mansion at King's House.

Together we stood on the sidewalk—my white family from the neo-Tudor house and our African servants who lived in the concrete shed at the far end of our garden. Our faces to the street, our backs to the house, we stood and waited. It was my father who'd gathered us, who told us, white and Black, adults and children, to witness and remember this day—historic for the Empire, for colonialism, for Africa, for South Africa, and for our family.

I didn't, then, understand anything about the event or what it signified, but my father did. His gravity, his injunction that we *must remember* so impressed me that the sight entered my consciousness and lodged there.

Macmillan's drive past our house was a late passage in a journey that began on January 5, 1960, when the PM departed London for a historic and unprecedented tour of Britain's African colonies. Macmillan, a pragmatist, wanted Britain out of Africa, for British imperialism was under attack and in retreat. His tour began in Ghana, continued to Nigeria, then to the Federation of Rhodesia and Nyasaland, and climaxed in the Union of South Africa.

Late January to February are Durban's hottest weeks. My mother, careful to safeguard her skin from the sun's damaging rays, never went out in the midday sun, especially not at that time of year. Yet that day she stood with us, un-hatted, her lacquered bouffant beehive glistening; we wore our finest clothes; our servants' uniforms were new. It was the same all along the route: Families like mine, Anglophiles, eager to demonstrate our devotion to Englishness, our loyalty to Crown and Commonwealth, stood with our servants. Yes, it was hot, but for the sake of the Empire we endured the heat.

First, we heard the shouts of our neighbors as the cavalcade neared, then the throaty thrum of the advance-guard police motorcade, and then we saw them: motorcyclists with giant Union Jacks that billowed, fluttered, and swelled in the gentle breeze, and, in an open limousine, Mr. Macmillan and Lady Dorothy. Energetically we waved. With due reserve, the distinguished couple—he in a pinstripe suit, she, hatted and in queenly pastel, dressed for London, not Durban—waved back. Their waves were slow and weary, the gestures of dignitaries who'd been waving for hours, for weeks, mile after slow mile down the vast expanse of Africa, graciously accepting the tributes of the imperial subjects they were about to abandon.

We thought they were waving hello. We were wrong. It was a farewell. Britain was done with us.

From Durban, Macmillan flew to Cape Town to address both Houses of Parliament. This last stop was fraught. According to contemporary accounts, Macmillan was so anxious about the speech he would deliver that he vomited in the men's room right before giving it.

Regardless, the speech that followed has entered the annals of history as "The Wind of Change" speech. In Etonian English, in language steeped in the classics, he informed his listeners: "The wind of change is blowing through this continent ... a wind of black nationalism." His subtext: Britain, buffeted and unable to withstand the wind, was withdrawing from her colonies. And then, with impeccable British politeness, in complex prose, Macmillan delivered his punch line—a critique of apartheid:

"... I hope you won't mind my saying frankly that there are some aspects of your policies that make it impossible for us to [give you our support] without being false to our own deep convictions about the political destinies of free men to which in our own territories we are trying to give effect."

South African Prime Minister Hendrick Verwoerd, chief architect of apartheid, *did* mind. Outraged, he sprang to his feet. "There must," he said, "be just[ice also] for the white man in Africa.... We call ourselves European, but actually we represent the white men of Africa.... We in this southernmost portion of Africa have such a stake here that this is our only motherland, and we have nowhere else to go."

My father did not, and never would, identify with the collective *we* of Verwoerd's response. South Africa was not *our* motherland, not our *home*; we did not share Verwoerd's nationalistic white supremacist stake in the country. We would find somewhere else to go, someplace else to call home.

The encounter with Macmillan emboldened Verwoerd. The government held a referendum—restricted to whites—to decide whether South Africa should become a republic. English-speaking

South Africans were outnumbered and outvoted, though the vote was narrow: 52.29 percent in favor of a republic. Verwoerd withdrew South Africa from the Commonwealth, freeing the apartheid government to pursue its policies without oversight from Whitehall and positioning South Africa as the world's pariah nation.

The year was choked with civil rights violations and widespread fear: the Cato Manor riots, the government banning of the ANC; police opening fire on a peaceful protest in Sharpville, killing sixty-nine; public meetings banned; a state of emergency declared in eighty magisterial districts; the United Nations Security Council condemning South Africa; an attempt made on the life of Verwoerd by a white farmer; 18,000 people arrested and detained; Black students barred from attending white universities; tribal clashes in Pondoland ... and on and on and on.

Despite this deluge of bad news, the economy boomed. Britain, needing South Africa's vast mineral resources, did not boycott South African goods or impose sanctions. Nonetheless, English-speaking South Africans felt betrayed, abandoned, and more out of place than ever before.

And still we did not leave. The economy buoyant, my father was poised for financial success, and so he deferred our departure from a country that was neither motherland nor home.

My anxiety about home, my longing for it, deepened. I grew more fearful, more reclusive, buried my nose in Victorian literature and dreamed of a world where our daily newspapers did not bear headlines of horror.

I don't know if these three moments—my father's talk quayside, my shock at seeing men running and calling for freedom outside my house, and Macmillan waving goodbye—were truly pivotal for me. When I lived through them, they were part of the ongoing continuum of my life. They have in retrospect become pivotal, moments from which I now plot the trajectory of my life story. Perhaps I have, over the years, read too much fiction and too many essays on the craft of fiction to be innocent of the urge to hinge a narrative for myself from what I now, decades later, identify as key memories. Perhaps they *were* key. Or have I snatched them from the phantasmagoria of memories, even embellished them, to make a coherent story of my life?

4

Girlhood to Young Adulthood

MUSGRAVE ROAD

THERE WERE, OF COURSE, THINGS THAT SEEMED ORDINARY AND everyday in that house on Musgrave Road: meals, bedtimes, school, homework, reading. But now I think that none of it was ordinary because everything was fraught with the country's complex history and its regime of apartheid.

Take, for example, our house, whose style—Neo-Tudor—was popular with English-speaking South Africans, the white majority in Natal. Far-flung from the imperial seat that, before South Africa left the Commonwealth, governed our colonial lives, English speakers embraced Tudor architecture as we did everything English. English was our mother tongue, the language we dreamed in, the language of the books and histories we identified with, the language we spoke with our friends, the language our parents spoke with us—though not always the language their parents had spoken with them. English was our self-conception, our identity. We fetishized and revered Englishness with the pathologically nostalgic longing of the chronically homesick—even if we'd never been to that longed-for homeland. It was our Shangri-La.

But in subtropical Durban, Tudor was an absurd architectural style, an out-of-place style. This made it perfect for a family whose paterfamilias aspired to be elsewhere and conveyed that aspiration to his children. It was an out-of-place house for an out-of-place family.

Out of place, yes, but it was home, and I loved it with the intensity that Gaston Bachelard, that great poet of domestic interiors, articulates so exquisitely in his *Poetics of Space*. Though I would not read Bachelard until decades later, when I eventually did, I was immediately transported back to the house on Musgrave Road. Though it was, in retrospect, *pokey*, with small rooms, some of them dark and, in my parents' view, not sufficiently spacious for a growing family of increasing affluence, for me it meant home and I was—and remain—deeply attached to all the spaces it held. To this day I can recall each vividly, from the lowest point: a tiny half-subterranean half bathroom where my father relieved himself in the mornings, to the pitched ceilings in the upstairs bedrooms that seemed to a small supine girl as lofty as the highest arch in a Gothic cathedral would have to an awestruck, upward-gazing medieval congregant.

Though I loved the house and cried when my parents told me we were leaving it for one larger and more modern where I'd have my own bedroom—something I longed for—it also held terrors—at least for a child with a too-active imagination nurtured on the tales of Poe and the haunting graveyard opening of Dickens's *Great Expectations*.

At night the wooden beams, wooden staircase, wooden floors, wooden front door, and wood-framed windows creaked. When my parents were out for dinner with friends and our nanny Dora was taking care of us, I'd lie still and listen anxiously to the speaking house. The creaks sounded like footsteps telling me an intruder had broken in and would creep upstairs and slit our throats, Dora's too, as she dozed beside us. I'd imagine my parents returning to find their children murdered, their nanny bleeding to death beside the mutilated bodies of her charges.

Looking up at the pitched ceiling, rigid with tension, I'd watch the shadows and listen for the sounds of a prowler. When I could no longer contain my apprehension, conscious that I, the oldest, almost ten, had responsibilities to my siblings, I'd get out of bed, stomp loudly on each wooden step, bang on the walls, fling open doors, and turn on all the lights to dazzle and shock the intruder into fleeing.

No one ever did break in, but I never stopped being afraid that someone would, for I'd inhaled the miasma of white fear that apartheid dispersed like a toxic virus across the land.

Dora said they were her brothers, the men who came one night when my parents were out at the home of friends.

I heard voices, Dora's and the voices of men, though the sounds were soft and low as though trying not to disturb sleeping children. I lay in the darkness listening, uncertain if the voices were a dream or coming from real people. At last, unable to bear not knowing, I could stay in bed no longer.

Barefoot, I descended the dark wooden stairs. A light shone in the crack beneath the kitchen door. Grasping the handle, I pushed it open.

A man was half lying, half sitting on the kitchen floor. His head drooped onto his chest and he looked as though he'd fainted. Two men knelt beside him, Dora too. He was bleeding and they were trying to help him, but they couldn't stop the blood that seeped through his khaki pants and made a dark pool on the white linoleum floor.

"I'll call an ambulance," I said, automatically assuming the role of white-person-taking-charge.

"No!" Dora said. "No! My brother, he no have passbook. Big trouble no passbook. You no call!"

She grasped my arm. It hurt. She'd never been angry with me

before. How could she be angry? The man needed help. He needed bandages.

I knew my mother kept two boxes of narrow padded bandages in her special drawer in the bathroom. When I'd asked what they were for, she got cross and said, "For bleeding, and you're too young to know about it." But now someone was bleeding and I knew about it, so I ran upstairs and brought an unopened box to the kitchen. Dora took it and told me to go to bed and not tell my parents about the men. I didn't want to leave, but I didn't want to make her angrier, so I went upstairs.

Lying in the dark, I listened to the sounds of Zulu from the kitchen. After a while I heard the kitchen door click shut and the house grow silent. I waited for Dora to come upstairs so I could ask if the man was all right, but she took so long that my eyes closed and I fell asleep.

The following morning when I went down for breakfast, the floor was as white and clean as if there'd never been a pool of blood spreading a dark stain across the whiteness.

I kept my promise to Dora and never told my parents.

I have another memory of that kitchen, one older than the one above. Its spectral shadows shimmer on the far edge of memory: color, light, skin a shade of milky coffee, gleaming copper, silver, and brass, blue jacaranda blossoms, dappled shadow.

Fikele sits on a spread of newspaper on the linoleum floor. He rests his back against the jamb of the door that opens to a covered alcove. From it, three steps descend to the garden path that leads to *ikhaya*—the concrete shed where our servants live at the far end of our garden behind the screen of the giant Amatangulu hedge. A late afternoon breeze enters through the door and windows. My mother, out playing bridge, will not be home until dinner and so the atmosphere is relaxed and happy.

Fikele's friend is visiting, squatting in the alcove with a tin mug of sweet tea from Miriam, who is also drinking tea, enjoying a break from her work at the stove, cooking chicken and potatoes for our dinner and *putu* with long-stewed "boy's meat" for herself, Dora, Fikele, and, most likely, Fikele's friend. The men chat softly in Zulu, the clicks and long vowels a familiar and reassuring sound, though I understand almost nothing of their meaning.

Fikele wears khaki shorts; his skin is the color of milky coffee, lighter than Miriam's, lighter than his friend's. His legs are bent, his feet are bare; his toes spread wide on the floor. My mother's silver tray rests on his thighs. He supports it with one hand. In the other he holds a rag. He is polishing the silver, the brass, and the copper. The pieces lie on the newspaper: a silver teapot, a silver coffeepot, a milk pitcher, Kiddush cups, spoons, trays, copper pots, a brass kettle, little teaspoons, large serving spoons. The Brasso tin of polishing fluid, its red center emblazoned with the red-and-white sunburst Brasso logo, is between his shins.

Cross-legged on the floor, my Shirley Temple doll in my lap, my cocker spaniel Sally beside me, I watch Fikele transform silver, copper, and brass from dull to iridescent while jacaranda blossoms drift downward past the window.

Here's another memory that won't let me go.

I'm sitting on the floor of the bedroom I share with my sister, reading. My Shirley Temple doll, the only doll I ever loved because she was my mother's when she was a child and I'm sentimental, is on my lap.

My mother appears in the doorway.

"Go to *ikhaya*," she says, "and tell Dora I need her."

"It's her 'off,'" I say, "and you told me I'm not allowed to go there."

"And now I'm telling you to go. Be quick."

"Why can't she have her 'off'?"

"She didn't finish her work. Go."

Clutching Shirley, I walk down the long garden path to *ikhaya*, turning right behind the Amatangulu hedge, past our laundry hanging on the clothesline—sheets, towels, my father's shirts and underwear, my little brother's clothes, my and my sister's frocks—to *ikhaya*. The Amatangulu hedge—straight and smooth and trim from the side we see from our house— is wild here, and the ground—soft and grassy on our side—is wet and weedy.

Which is Dora's door?

I hear low voices, a man's and a woman's, behind the middle one. I knock.

"Dora? Dodie? It's me."

The voices grow silent. The air fills with the sounds of cicadas, vibrations of a mating symphony. The sound wraps around *ikhaya*, around Shirley and me.

A woman opens the door. She wears a thin dress torn at the pocket and shoulder, the hem frayed and uneven. Her feet are bare. Her head is bare. I see her hair: short, tufty, black with flecks of gray.

"Dora?"

Dora always wears a pale green uniform, starched, with a white apron, also starched, tied at her back; her hair is always covered by a *doek*; she always wears shoes, black and thick-soled.

"Dora?"

Through the half-open door I see a room illuminated by a bare light bulb on a wire, a pair of shoes—black and thick-soled—placed neatly against the wall, and above, on a wire hanger hooked over a nail, a pale green uniform. The only furniture is an iron bed raised on bricks so the evil *tokoloshe* can't reach up and grab the dreaming sleeper's soul. On the bed is a man.

"Wut, Miss Jo-Anne," the woman says. "Why you here? Wut you want? This my off. My wuk, she done. You mother, she no like you come *ikhaya*. Why you here?"

"I'm sorry," I say. "My mother sent me. She says she needs you."

"You go," she says. "You tell you mother this my off."

Next day, when I return from school, I cannot find Dora.

"Where is she?" I ask my mother.

"Gone. There are plenty of girls who'd love this job. The new girl starts tomorrow."

Reliving the event as I write, I am moved to find a photograph of Dora in one of my mother's albums when next I visit. I'm sure there is one. I remember seeing one. But I'm wrong. There is no photograph *of* Dora, though there's one that *includes* her. Part of her.

The photo shows children at a table festooned with streamers, balloons, plates of half-eaten birthday cake, and melting ice cream. Behind each child stands her nanny. There is a nanny behind me. I know it is Dora, can recall beneath the starch of her pale green uniform the full softness of her belly and the pendulous droop of her breasts. Only her body is included. The photographer, who would have been my grandfather, did not include Dora's face in the frame. It is I who am framed—a small white child against the body of her Black nanny.

For whatever reasons—and they are not clear to me—I filed these memories of Dora and Fikele; and for whatever reasons they have surfaced from the ocean of oblivion into which experience sinks. For whatever reason they have called to me. I don't know what to do with them other than own them in their fraught complexity.

Not Learning Afrikaans

South Africa's racial and racist issues were compounded by a language issue. This, effectively, amounted to a war between the two white language groups: English and Afrikaans. Slightly less than half of South Africa's white population was in love with everything English. The other half—the Afrikaans-speaking majority—was deeply, intensely Anglophobic. The resentment went back to the 1830s, when Dutch-descended farmers, Boers, trekked north into the hinterland to escape the governance of the British, who acquired the colony in 1806 after the start of the Napoleonic Wars and whose values, including slave emancipation, the burghers did not share.

Mutual antagonisms took a deep dive with the Anglo-Boer Wars (1899–1902) when the British, lusting after the rich mineral deposits of gold and diamonds in the newly established Boer Republics of the Transvaal and Orange Free State, went to war with the Boers. Five hundred thousand British soldiers fought 88,000 Boers. The latter, who knew the country intimately, were initially successful until Britain, humiliated, adopted a scorched-earth policy—burning Boer farmlands and placing Boer women and children in concentration camps, where approximately 27,000 died of starvation and typhoid. The exhausted Boers capitulated. The war ended in 1902, but Afrikaner hatred and resentment of the British endured, particularly among Boer women, some of whom swore they would never permit their children to speak English.

Although the two sides laid down their arms and agreed to stop killing one another, the war of language and culture continued. Many English-speakers regarded Afrikaners with contempt, dismissing their language as a form of pidgin Dutch, their Calvinism as anachronistically fundamentalist, and their politics as stuck in a nineteenth-century slaveholders' mentality. For their part, Afrikaners were determined to maintain their language, church, morals, and habits. In 1910, when the Union of South Africa was created from the separate colonies of the Cape, the Transvaal, the Orange Free State, and Natal, Article 137 of the Union Constitution decreed, "Both the English and Dutch [Afrikaans] languages shall be official languages of the Union and shall be treated on a footing of equality...."

Legislation notwithstanding, the two white language groups remained separate and mutually suspicious. As an English speaker, I resented and resisted having to study Afrikaans because it was more than a language; it was an ideology and the medium of the administration of apartheid.

In my Anglo-dominant province of Natal, in my Anglo-dominant town of Durban, I almost never encountered Afrikaners. The only Afrikaner woman I ever knew was Mevrou Bezeidenhout, who taught Afrikaans at my (very) English girls' school. And the only reason she was there was because all schools for white children were required to include at least one class in the other official language.

I remember her well: tall, heavyset, gray-haired, stern, her voice guttural, her head held high. Though I disliked her, I now think of her with empathy. How difficult it must have been for her to be the only Afrikaner in an English-medium school, where she must have felt our disdain for her language and culture and where her strong Afrikaans accent marked her as not belonging. I should have empathized with her for I too was an outsider. The school's official denomination was Church of England; Jewish students were admitted on a quota system, and "excused" at Easter and Christmas from participating in festival-specific events. From elementary through high school, it was as though I had a yellow Star of David pinned to my bottle-green uniform announcing, *This student does not belong*. I belonged as little as Mev. Bezeidenhout.

What I most remember about her classes are not grammar drills and vocabulary tests but the time she caught me reading a book on my lap when she was teaching. Perhaps she thought I meant to insult her by reading an English book in her Afrikaans class, but it was probably boredom or not understanding her Afrikaans words— or not wanting to—that led me to slide my hand under the lid of my desk and pull out a paperback edition of Dreiser's *An American Tragedy*. I remember the cover as clearly as if I were holding it right now: an artist's rendition of a couple, clearly lovers, on a small boat against a black background—an illustration of the novel's central drama. If the viewer knew nothing of the story, she might think it betokened a lurid narrative.

Wholly absorbed in the tragedy unfolding on my knees, I was unaware that Mev. Bezeidenhout was standing at my right shoulder until she yanked the book from my lap, held it aloft, and challenged me to tell the class, in Afrikaans, what I was reading.

I wanted to tell her that I was reading a great novel by a great American writer, but I was stutter prone, particularly in Afrikaans, whose guttural sounds my mouth balked at shaping; and I lacked the vocabulary to rise to her challenge. Nevertheless, silent, I felt morally superior because I, an English speaker, was reading a great book in a great language whose illustrious canon Afrikaans could not equal.

I was at fault, not Mev. Bezeidenhout, but the incident left me even more resistant to Afrikaans, more incapable of uttering its sounds and mastering its grammar—though it is much easier for a native English speaker than Latin, French, Italian, or German, all of which I would later study with pleasure.

Afrikaans felt like a hurdle, a block that would forever hold me back. For decades, before any major event stressor in which I would, in some way, be put to a test—the deposition for my divorce, the US Citizenship Test, the German language requirement for my PhD advancement to candidacy, certification to become a yoga instructor—I dreamed I had failed Afrikaans.

Though Mev. Bezeidenhout almost certainly had no connection to the South African Censorship Board, the image of her holding my book aloft and her fury that I was reading it, became, for me, the personification of that board—arbiter of what great classics I might and might not read: *Lady Chatterley's Lover, Tropic of Capricorn, Lolita, The Story of O*—forbidden lest they lure innocents like me down a path to perdition. I resented that Afrikaners, with their young, almost nonexistent literary tradition, stood as gatekeepers between me and the books I yearned to read—yearned with an especial intensity because *they* wouldn't let me access them.

Mangoes

Another memory insistently surfaces. This one's personal, not recorded in the roster of historic events. But, like so much that's personal, it could only have happened in apartheid South Africa. Like the previous three events, it made such an indelible impression that I am compelled to include it in my narrative of formative experiences.

In 1969, nineteen years old, in my second year at university, back in Durban for a midterm break, I attended a mixed-race party in Chatsworth Indian township on the outskirts of Durban. I don't recall how I learned about the party—probably from one of the girls at my white liberal university in Johannesburg.

We went to transgress with Indian boys. The Indian boys came to transgress with us.

I lied to my parents about where I was going. Correction: I gave them a partial truth:

"I'm going out with friends."

"All right," said my father. "You know the rules: Wake me when you get home."

I hated that rule, but I followed it.

Taboo and risk framed the event: The Immorality Amendment Act of 1950 and the more finely calibrated Sexual Offenses Act of 1957 made sexual contact between a white person and a person of another race illegal and punishable.

In my thin cotton dress I stood, awkward, in the small living room of a Chatsworth matchbox house. Chatsworth was for Indians and Indians only. No other racial group could live there. White visitors to Chatsworth were conspicuous.

We had giggled, my friends and I, in the Indian taxi that had brought us to this house, giggled from the frisson of danger, excitement, and fear.

Now, nervous, I hovered at the drinks table. I wanted alcohol, *needed* alcohol, to take the edge off my anxiety. Our host, Amichandi, chatting and laughing, dispensed fruity orange punch from a large bowl with a plastic ladle. I extended my plastic cup. Careful not to spill, he filled it, and I, eager for a quick rush of alcohol-induced dulling, for something to move me beyond my frightened thrill about this forbidden mixed-race party in this four-room, semidetached house more spartan than any I'd ever entered, gulped it down.

In the days leading up to the party I'd fantasized about it, imagined myself flirting and laughing; but now the time had come to flirt and laugh, and I was incapable of either. Chronically shy, engaging with young men was difficult for me, and this evening was fraught beyond any I'd hitherto spent with members of the opposite sex.

Ordinarily sensitive to alcohol's effects, I felt nothing from the drink, no fuzzy stupor to buffer my growing sense of awkwardness and out-of-placeness. I felt I'd been wrong to come, wrong to have entertained a transgressive thrill at the prospect of interracial mixing. Now, uncertain how to comport myself, wishing I were anywhere else, I focused on the marigold mango slice at the bottom of my cup, wondering if its flaccid half-moon had absorbed whatever alcohol had once laced the punch and if I should try to get it out and eat it.

"I wouldn't bother fishing it out," a voice said. "There's almost no alcohol in the punch or the mango. The penalty for mixed-race drinking is almost as severe as the penalty for sex, and alcohol's easier to detect. Besides, the mango won't taste any good. It's been too long in sugared juice, though when fresh it's wonderful."

He startled me, this tall young man with thick glasses and large ears. How long had he been standing there watching my awkward efforts at extricating a limp slice of mango?

"I love mangoes," I said. "They're my favorite fruit."

"It's from the garden, from the tree you can see through that window."

He spoke with an accent more British than Durban Indian—at least the Durban Indians I'd met: waiters at hotels and restaurants, employees at my father's factory, Indian vendors of fruits and vegetables, or the samosa lady at her small kiosk downtown—and with far more self-assurance. Yet he was talking about fruit. Indians and fruit were an association I understood. Indians were Durban's market gardeners. Cato Manor had once been a fertile farmland where Indian banana growers and market gardeners had cultivated ginger, garlic, sweet potatoes, rice, lychees, mangoes, and flowers on small plots. Going "to the Indian" to buy fruit was part of the vernacular of Durbanites, both white and Black. And that accent?

"The cultivar is Raspuri," he continued. "Amichandi's sister grew it from a seed in Cato Manor. When the government kicked them out, she dug the little tree out of their garden and planted it here. Now, as you see, it's a big tree. There's a ladder against the trunk. Before you leave, we can check to see if there are any ripe ones for you to take home. Amichandi won't mind."

He extended his hand. "I'm Dan Motala."

My hand was damp. I set down the cup, wiped my hand on my dress, and shook his.

"Jo-Anne," I said.

"Would you like to dance?"

"Mr. Tambourine Man" was on the turntable.

Of course I wanted to dance. It was the reason I'd come. To feel an Indian boy's body against mine, to close my eyes against color and phenotype, to taste forbidden fruit.

Two or three couples moved against one another in the boxlike space—bare save for a folding table on which sat the bowl with its residue of punch and, in a corner on the floor, a turntable with a low pile of records beside it.

Dan Motala drew me to him. I rested my cheek against his jacket lapel, trying to feel his Indian-ness, his different-ness. But all I got was the fabric's roughness against my skin, the boniness of his breastplate, a faint dankness from his armpit, and the mismatching of height that kept my cheek from his. I wanted him to press his pelvis against me, to feel our bodies shift from the tension of white against brown to the molten state of girl-and-boy, to feel that he shared my terror and desire for intimacy. But his embrace was formal, a convention of the two-step, and his body deliberately distant.

Amichandi tapped him on the shoulder.

"*Bhai*," Amichandi said, "in a half hour the girls have to leave. I'm calling two taxis. They took too long to get here. My sister will be home soon. We have to clean up and move the furniture back in."

"Let's see about those mangoes," said Dan Motala.

I followed him down three concrete steps into the darkening garden where a couple, leaning into the wall at the far side of the house, was kissing. I wanted Dan to kiss me, to hold me close so our hands could wander over each other in search of skin where color disappeared. But he stepped onto the first rung of the ladder, his back to me, and examined the fruit hanging from the branches.

"They're too green," he said. "Not ripe enough to pick. Sorry about that. It'll be a while before the taxis get here. Why don't we sit and chat?"

He seated himself on the second step. I sat beside him, our closeness an effect of the narrowness of the step, not his desire.

He was, he told me, studying in England—initially at public school, now at the London School of Economics—and was back in Durban briefly to visit his parents. They were Gujarati, part of an old Gujarati merchant diaspora with family in Manchester and London. He was engaged to an English girl he'd met at university and was going to marry her and make England his home because she was white and interracial marriage in South Africa was illegal under the Prohibition of Mixed Marriages and Group Areas Acts.

A wave of loss engulfed me. What rotten luck to have been asked to dance by someone already committed to another—and a white girl at that! From the moment I'd been included in this secret excursion into Chatsworth Township, I'd been unable to think of anything else. It had consumed my fantasy life. In the days leading up to this evening, anticipating it, I'd lain awake in the darkness in my women's residence dorm and fantasized the evening that was yet to come: I would sacrifice my virginity to an Indian boy in the cause of the antiapartheid struggle; the riskiness of our mating would intensify and sweeten our embraces; defying the law of the land, our passion overshadowing our caution, we'd fall in love, risking banning orders, confiscation of our passports, or the issuance of exit-only passports that would disallow return to our homeland; we would become heroes, martyrs in the cause; our names would enter the historical record as the Romeo and Juliet of the apartheid struggle . . . and on and on, until, at last, exhausted, I drifted into troubled sleep.

My wave of loss was followed by overwhelming relief. At heart I was timid, a "good girl" not disposed to transgression and relieved to be spared the passionate adventures of my fantasies. It must have been written all over me—my good-girl-ness, my Goody Two-shoes-ness—standing there at the drinks table, fixated on a flabby slice of mango at the bottom of my cup. The bespoken Dan had seen it. How could anyone miss it!

"And anyway," he said, "my father wants us all to leave. It's rough for Indians here. We're in the middle. Whites keep passing legislation to deny us opportunities, and Africans want to drive us out or kill us. It's impossible. My brother's just graduated from medical school in London. He won't be coming back. What about you?"

I wanted to tell him we were going to leave too, that my father had been telling me since I was a child to make myself "exportable," that I must stop thinking of South Africa as home because he'd made up his mind to get us all out before the inevitable bloodbath of revenge against whites: "far worse," he'd always say, "than the Mau Mau's bloody retributions in Kenya."

But I was crying. It took me by surprise. The lump in my throat. My quivering lower lip. I tried suppressing it, but that made it worse.

"I'm sorry," I said. "I cry easily."

"It's OK. There's plenty to cry about."

I bit my lower lip to stop the quivering.

"I'm second year at Wits," I said. "Art history and English literature. My father told me to make myself 'exportable' so I can leave and get a job and make a home someplace else. I doubt literature and art history will help with that, but they're what I love. I *want* to leave. I think about it all the time. But my father says we don't have the resources. Not yet. We don't have connections overseas, except my grandfather's sister in London, and she's old and Grandpa supports her."

It was early evening. The late afternoon sun had baked the steps, the wall of the house behind us, and the corrugated iron roof. Their surfaces held on to the heat. I was glad of the warmth, for I'd begun to shiver in my thin cotton dress, though my shivering had little to do with the thinness of the fabric. Internally generated, it spread from my core to my skin, producing goose bumps and making the fine hairs on my arms stand up. Shivering, I hunched over, wrapping my arms about myself, rocking back and forth until self-consciousness made me stop.

Dan seemed warm. Beads of sweat glistened on his forehead, and he took off his jacket, folding it inside out at the apex, extending it across his knees, exposing the lining and the label on the inside breast pocket.

The label. It startled me. *Man About Town.* My father's line of menswear, produced at his factory where 2,600 Indians, men and women, worked at cutting tables and sewing machines, turning out 2,400 pants and 1,500 jackets every day.

I turned my head to look at Dan. Had he exposed the label to let me know he knew my father was Man About Town? He was stroking the silky lining, smoothing it across his thighs to take out the creases. He seemed oblivious to the label, but I could not pull my eyes from it. The radio ad, which my father had taken to whistling and my siblings and I to singing, played in my head:

Man About Town, Man About Town,

> *Dressed for success in the suit of renown,*
> *Wonderful things happen to a Man About Town.*

I shook my head to get rid of the ditty, but it wouldn't leave. I didn't want to hear it, didn't, at that moment, want anything to do with Man About Town. I felt as though my father had interposed himself between my cheek and Dan's, as though the fabric of Dan's jacket—which my father would have selected from a textile mill in Germany or Manchester, as he did all his cloth—had been a paternal interdiction against the intimacy I sought—or thought I sought—with a young Indian man. It was as though my father were here, watching, making sure his daughter observed the law of the land—though he disagreed with that law and warned me not to think of that land as "home." In that moment, shivering and disappointed, I felt my father as an agent, or extension, of the government's panoptic regulative gaze, felt him as the embodiment of the paternalistic superego that South Africans—that I—had internalized so I could be a good girl and stay out of trouble so I could leave and start my real life somewhere else. I told myself that I was stupid, stupid, stupid, and a coward. The girls I'd come with were necking and petting, but I sat on a step, hugging myself, crying, and feeling the presence of my father.

Amichandi stood in the doorway.

"Time to say bye-bye," he said. "The taxis are here."

When I returned home there was no evading my father's iron rule for a daughter who'd been out at night: awaken him and let him know I was home.

I pushed open my parents' bedroom door and stood beside my father in the darkness. I didn't want to awaken him, but, mindful of his insistence that I do, reached my hand down and lightly touched his chest.

"I'm awake," he said, "I couldn't sleep until I knew you were home. I hope you had a good time."

I wanted to scream, *But I'm NOT home! And you're the one who told me I'm not. No one is home in this hateful country.* But I said, "Yes, yes. I had a good time."

"Good girl," he said. "Now go to bed and let me rest."

Love and Letters

Not long thereafter I found the love I'd sought in Chatsworth. It happened with a man almost as far outside my comfort zone as any of the young men in Chatsworth, was almost as much a fantasy, and was almost equally doomed by my too-conventional, too-middle-class self to sustain.

The man I fell in love with—I'll call him Steven—was my first lover and, on that account, unforgettable. I even kept the letters he wrote to me when, in 1970, I went on an overseas art tour because I and my parents wanted me to connect with cultures more urbane and sophisticated than ours. I have them still. When I left on the trip, Steven and I had been together for a week and were in the first flush of love.

We'd met on the steps of the library at Wits. As I climbed the steps, preoccupied about a research paper I had yet to begin, I was startled by a sudden cackle—high-pitched, staccato, almost manic. I stopped to see its source: a small odd-looking man talking with someone I knew. I went up to them; I felt I didn't have a choice; something about him compelled me. He was, he said, in the MA program in philosophy; I told him I was an undergraduate in English literature and art history. He asked me out and I said yes.

Later in the day, I had an appointment with one of my professors, the son of a famous South African novelist.

"We're having a party at my house tonight," he said. "Come if you're free."

"I have a date with Steven R," I said, thinking he might know Steven. In those days there weren't sharp boundaries between MA students and faculty—most of whom didn't have PhDs. Apparently, given the invitation, there weren't inhibiting boundaries between faculty and undergraduates either.

"Steven R?" said the son of the famous South African novelist. "Steven likes to party. Bring him. Have you heard about our parties?"

"No."

"Now's the time. Think of it as part of your education."

I was committed to my education.

I tracked Steven down at a carrel in the library and told him about the party.

His high-pitched cackle shattered the library's hushed silence.

"Let's do it!" he said.

A sweet, spicy smell with hints of anise, orange, and lemon greeted us at the open front door of our host's house.

"There's a bag of Durban Poison on the table," someone called out. "Feel free to roll yourselves a couple."

"Crystal Blue Persuasion" was on the turntable. The professor with whom I was taking a class on D. H. Lawrence was dancing with a girl from the class, his face nuzzled into her neck, his hands under her shirt, stroking her back. The son of the famous South African novelist was dancing with a girl from my romantic poetry class, his hands on her buttocks as they hip-synched to the music, his wife glowering at a distance.

Steven and I shared a joint and danced. Then everyone went out to the pool and took off their clothes. Some, not yet ready to relinquish their Styrofoam cups of red wine or another puff on the thick joints doing the rounds, lay down on plastic lawn chairs. Others jumped into the pool. Steven too. Soon only I and an older woman in a Laura Ashley granny print dress still had our clothes on—allies in decorum at the side of the pool.

I didn't want to be her ally. Quickly, I pulled off my top and jeans.

"Yes!" I heard someone cry. "Jo-Anne's taken her clothes off!"

I jumped in. Over the splash I heard that crazy cackle.

He was different from the young men my parents had in mind for me: boys in medical school eager for a professional, grown-up life with a pretty wife and adorable kids; or the econ majors ambitious for entrepreneurial adventures or remaking the family business. Steven didn't conform to those pictures. He didn't fit, and I, hiding behind my reserve, felt I didn't either.

In the four months that we were a couple, I never heard him speak of his parents. It was as though he didn't have any, and I envied him his tabula rasa, the freedom that not belonging to anyone or anything seemed to give him. It was as though, like his laugh, he'd erupted—idiosyncratic and fully himself—onto the library steps where I'd encountered him.

His field was analytic philosophy, which, as I understood, probed the limits of logic. The subject of his thesis was "the bottomless pit." The aporia fascinated and amused him. Whenever he spoke of it, that wild, crazy cackle erupted out of him.

What did he look like?

His hair was close-cropped, almost military—an abjuration of the current vogue for hippie shoulder-length locks; and he was never not clean-shaven. It struck me that his mind was Athenian and his body Spartan: small, compactly muscled, finely drawn, neat and contained, save for the electricity that vibrated out of him in a kind of static. He'd let out that crazy laugh, his pupils dilating, then narrowing into pinpricks, as though he saw something the rest of us weren't privy to. He had a supercharged sensuality; his lovemaking was of a piece with that: a crazy intensity, a leap into an impossible space, then back to earth again.

I was madly in love.

At every city my tour group visited, there was a letter waiting for me, and every day I wrote to him. When I reread his, it's easy to see how ill-suited we were.

"Marriage," he wrote, "is a bourgeois institution. Kierkegaard wouldn't marry the woman he loved until she overcame her bourgeois self. She never did and eventually married a banker, a good investment." And: "There is only one kind of successful revolution—to overthrow your old self—which means you'll suffer and be lonely and without a country to call home."

In addition to his letters—which unsettled, intrigued, and compelled me—I read books he gifted me before I left. "In case you get bored looking at great art," he'd said as he handed me a package that held Burroughs's *Naked Lunch*, Hesse's *Steppenwolf*, Joyce's *Portrait of the Artist as a Young Man*, and Huxley's *Brave New World*. Wanting to earn Steven's love, I put them in my luggage.

It was the first time I'd been so far from home, unmoored from family and country, every other day a different city, every day filled with a dizzying, overwhelming immersion in the vast galleries of Europe's greatest museum treasures, every night absorbed in the alien worlds of the books Steven had gifted me. I was exultant, feeling myself becoming as free as I imagined Steven was.

I loved the intellectual exchange of our letters, rich in Steven's comments about great thinkers from Plato to Nietzsche. I responded with observations from the books he'd given me. Though I don't have the letters I wrote to him, I know that mine were quick-witted and articulate in ways I didn't know how to be in South Africa. *There* I was earnest and worried. It was as though, abroad, I was the self I aspired to be, the self Steven wanted me to be.

Returned, I could not sustain that self. For his part, Steven could not sustain a relationship with flesh-and-blood, awkward, uncertain, and needy me. The end came when he revealed he'd been sleeping with my best friend's sister. I burst into tears.

"I thought we were a couple," I said.

"Being 'a couple,'" he said, "is a fantasy for timid fools."

He had my number. His attraction to a bottomless pit frightened me. I was not into free-fall. I craved solid ground into which I could sink roots. I needed connection.

After Steven left me, I met the man who became my husband. He wasn't a banker, but it was close: He had an MBA from Berkeley. Unlike Kierkegaard's lover's marriage, mine was a rotten investment.

I'll call him H. We began dating in 1971.

My great-aunt introduced us. She lived in the same northern suburb of Johannesburg and on the same leafy street as H's mother.

"He's from a good family," she'd said. "He's been in California for three years getting his MBA and then working for a prominent marketing firm. He's returned home to help run the family business. I think you'd be a good match."

My aunt put in a call to H's mother to arrange a meeting, then walked me to H's mother's house, and there was H—in the garden, clutching a large brown paper sack, bantering with the young African man who took care of the grounds. As you can probably tell by now, I'm drawn to odd-looking men. H met that criterion. He was lanky, mustached, with long stringy hair tied into a ponytail, dressed in worn blue jeans that hung low on narrow hips. When he spotted me at the far edge of the garden with my aunt, he crossed the wide expanse of lawn to greet us. When my aunt left, he opened the brown paper sack.

"The gardener's my source," he said. "It's good stuff." I bent to inhale its sweet piney fragrance and potent hit of cannabis dust. Perhaps, I thought, I could have both—a conventional middle-class life *and* countercultural frisson? Initially, it seemed I could. On our first dates, stoned, H regaled me with stories of living in a commune in San Carlos, California, with law school dropouts and activists and their adventures taking acid and piling into a friend's VW bus to drive to San Francisco to hear Janis Joplin, or Jefferson Airplane, or the Grateful Dead. His literary heroes were Norman Mailer, Tom Wolfe, and Hunter S. Thompson—more entertaining and a lot easier to read than the antiestablishmentarians in Steven's canon. H's conversation was as funny as he was funny-looking, especially when enhanced with the contents of the brown paper sack.

We became lovers, though I wasn't sure if I was in love with him or with the world he'd just left and spoke of with deep longing. Sunny, campy, and hedonistic, California seemed light-years from the oppressive bottomless pit of South African doom. Here, for example, are two South African tragedies that marked 1971, the year H and I met:

(1) Political detainee Ahmed Timol, a Muslim schoolteacher, allegedly jumped to his death from the tenth floor of the main police building in Johannesburg where he'd been detained for "questioning," bringing to seventeen the number of political detainees who'd perished under the watch of the police.

(2) Colored people (an official racial category in South Africa) were removed from the common voters' roll, thereby depriving them of rights they'd enjoyed for a hundred years.

My father was right: the country was impossible. We were all—Black and white—dehumanized by living there.

Though I'd always thought I'd leave South Africa for England, I found myself, after I met H, shifting my focus to California. The Golden State became my vision of a promised land. And so, Anglophile though I was, I switched the destination of my desire from England to California and the object of my passion from an analytic Marxist philosopher to a California wannabe with an MBA from Berkeley.

But within weeks of our meeting, my hippie cut his hair, stuffed his blue jeans into a drawer, put on a suit and tie, and assumed management, under his crochety bachelor uncle, of fifty-five family-owned clothing stores all over South Africa. He became irritable and moody, though sometimes, on weekends, a fat joint in one hand, a glass of Chablis in the other, the Grateful Dead on the turntable, his old self—the self I thought I was in love with, the self I hoped was his *real* self—returned. I attributed his shift from sunshine to gloom to the impossible and toxic world of South Africa. If only, I thought, if only I can get him back to California: The dark clouds will part, fair weather will prevail, and all will be well. Ah, the future tense, the mood of longing and expectation, the mood of accursed hope.

Weeks would pass and we would be intimate and loving, and I would be happy until, suddenly, for no reason I could discern, H would grow angry and withdrawn and not look at me, and I would be distraught and uncomprehending. Sometimes, after an eternity of days of withdrawal, he would tell me the cause: His uncle had been critical, or a friend had upset him, or—increasingly—it was me, he alleged, who'd said or done something egregious. In those days I knew nothing about mental health; now I would guess he had bipolar disorder. Though I never meant to offend and usually couldn't understand how I had, I always apologized, always took the blame. Over time I grew guarded lest I inadvertently trigger the dark mood of his anger and punishing retreat.

Epiphany

When I met H, I was living in a small flat in Hillbrow—a densely populated bohemian suburb on Jo'burg's east-west ridge. I took the flat for the view, which reached across the central business district to the squat block homes of Soweto to the gold mine waste dumps whose shapes—spectral in the dry, hazy distance—belied their primacy in generating Johannesburg, *Egoli*, City of Gold.

I loved that view as much for its Jo'burg-ness as for its differentness from my hometown—too lushly tropical, too caressingly humid, too gently undulant in its geography. What I didn't then understand was how much my flat's glorious horizontal vista was haunted by dreams and nightmares of verticality—both above and below ground—how scarred by death and greed. All I saw from my picture window was the pulsing metropolis of the day, the Turneresque landscape of dusk and, when night finally came with the suddenness that happens on the Highveld, a world as black as pitch that, in the blink of an eye, became a fairyland of twinkling lights.

I was, then, friends with a woman named Zoe. Tending, as I did in those days, to put people on a pedestal, I was in awe of Zoe, who seemed so much further along than I on whatever path I was trying to figure out I needed to be on. Already graduated from the art history program I was completing, she had a degree in psychotherapy and an MA in English literature from Cambridge University, England, where she'd had a glamorous-sounding nervous breakdown and an encounter with my hero, Doris Lessing. Now, back in Jo'burg to figure out her next chapter, she was working for a local left-wing women's paper for which she'd scored an interview with Winnie Mandela. I think I took her for a female version of Steven, for she was resolutely single, as dismissive as he of family, an intellectual, and a free spirit; and I, not yet done with the fantasy of Steven-like freedom, wanted to *be* her.

For her part, she assumed the role I assigned her, treating me like an ingenue in need of mentoring, though her actions often confused me: on greeting and parting she would kiss me softly on the mouth and hold me close, caressing my back, and then, releasing me, would first tousle, then pat smooth my hair as though I were a child; she'd close her eyes, smile, and let out her breath in a long, sonorous "Mmmmmnn." Androgynous in OshKosh B'Goshes, lanky, long-boned, languid in her movements, five-foot-eleven in Birkenstocks, she seemed to look down on me through her John Lennon spectacles; and I, five-foot-two, felt myself a hyperactive squat toad beneath her regard.

Her flat was one block from mine, and I visited often, especially when things had gone south with H and I was in want of comforting. On one such day when I was crying and blaming myself for having upset H for *something* that had sent him into a fury, she rose from the sofa, went into her kitchen, and returned with a small plastic bag containing three teensy foil-wrapped packages, each pinched tightly closed.

"It's LSD," she said. "Highest quality. Very pure. Take one when you need an epiphany. In my view, the sooner the better."

Drying my tears, I reached for the bag, accepting it gingerly with thumb and forefinger, at arm's length, as though it might at any moment explode into a blinding epiphany. Though I'd smoked cannabis, I'd never thought of trying LSD and wasn't sure, even with Zoe's encouragement, that I would. Nonetheless, compliant, I took the bag.

"I've been reading Timothy Leary," she explained. "He's a genius and a huge advocate of LSD. It's done wonders for me. You're the way I used to be: too much in your head, too buzzy with words. LSD will help you transcend verbal concepts. It will set you free."

She was probably right. Perhaps an epiphany—or three, if I used all the caps—was what I needed.

"Keep the caps in their foil in the freezer," she added. "They'll stay potent longer. When you do take one, let it dissolve slowly under your tongue. And be sure to have company. Someone you trust."

A few days later she was gone. Off to Esalen. The following month I received a letter from her:

Esalen's amazing! I lay naked on a massage table in a room full of people and, without anyone touching me or touching myself, had the greatest orgasm of my life.

In her absence I'd forgotten the acid caps hibernating in my freezer. Her letter reminded me that I possessed magic caps that could set me free.

I made myself a mug of tea and stood in front of the refrigerator—a little old one, like those in cheap motels, about hip height. Cupping the mug in both hands and bringing the hot tea to my mouth, I wished I'd asked Zoe for more information: How long would it take before an epiphany struck? How long would the epiphany last? Would I be all right?

Setting the half-empty mug on top of the refrigerator, I pulled open the door and then reached for the freezer door, pulled, then yanked, and yanked again. It had frozen solidly shut, for I'd not opened it since placing the caps there weeks ago. A moment before, I'd been ambivalent, but now frustration drove me forward. I boiled water in a large pot that I held as close to the freezer door as I could, then immersed a tea towel in hot water and held that against the stuck door. When it still wouldn't give, determined that nothing would come between me and an epiphany, I hacked at the ice with a small knife, managing to stab my hand. Wrapping my injury in a towel, I gave the door one more yank. It yielded.

Bending, I peered inside. There, on a metal ice tray, sat the plastic bag. Removing a single square of foil, unwrapping it, I placed a cap under my tongue and, to enhance the soluble environment in my mouth, took a swig of now cold tea. Twenty minutes passed. Nothing. I wandered to the window. Between my building and the five-hundred-foot drop from the Hillbrow escarpment into downtown stretched a small park—more a narrow strip of green about twelve feet wide and forty feet long than a park—just broad enough for two young jacaranda trees and a bench. Remembering Zoe's caveat about company, I reckoned I'd be better off in a public park than alone in my flat. And if no one came to the park? My eyes lit on George Eliot's *Daniel Deronda* sticking out of my bookshelf. I knew the book so well it *was* company. If no one came to the park I'd have Daniel and Gwendolen and Mirah by my side.

Locking the door to my flat, I descended the stairwell, *Daniel Deronda* in hand. On the second-floor landing I almost ran into Rosie, the African woman who cleaned the building. She was on hands and knees, scrubbing the steps.

"*Molo. Unjani*, Rosie," I said. Hello, how are you?

"*Molo. Phila enkosi.*" Hello, fine, thank you.

For a moment I thought of asking her to stay with me for the duration of my acid trip—if it ever happened—but I knew she had two more floors to clean and would not be done until evening, when she would make the long journey home to Soweto via two buses and a train on which *tsotsi* gangsters preyed on vulnerable commuters, and had two young sons to care for once she arrived home and a husband she worried would not come home because he was involved with the ANC and was probably under police surveillance. I felt ashamed to be waiting for an epiphany.

The park was empty. I sat down on the bench to one side, the book at my hip. Plenty of room should anyone come and, if I were lucky, sit beside me. After a while, I was about to give up and return to my flat when a man appeared at the park's far end. *Gentleman* is probably a better word, for everything about him spoke of a bygone era when *gentleman* was a visible attribute: his tweedy, worn, double-breasted jacket, his brown trousers, his heavy brown bluchers, his narrow mustache, his neat gray hair, his old-fashioned steel-rimmed owlish spectacles, his slow halting gait as he approached the bench.

Half facing me, half facing the bench, inclining his head politely, bringing his right hand across his torso as though to bow, he inquired, "Would you mind if I sat down and shared your bench?"

He had an accent I couldn't place. Eastern European?

"Please," I said, drawing George Eliot closer to make space.

Removing a large handkerchief from his jacket pocket, then unfolding it, he laid it on the bench, smoothed it flat, then sat on it, at the same time pinching and slightly lifting the pleat of his trousers at the knees, as I'd seen my grandfather do, to keep them from bagging. With a soft sigh, he leaned heavily into the backrest, which wobbled at the sudden weight of his round-shouldered back and drew his feet under the bench as though to hide their worn leather. Elderly, puffing slightly, he seemed in need of a rest. Pulling a second handkerchief from his trouser pocket, he dabbed at his forehead and mustache, then, noticing the book at my side, peered intently at its Penguin Classics cover through his owlish lenses.

Brightening, he said, "Ah! I see you're a serious reader." He lifted his gaze to mine, hesitated, then: "Might I inquire if you are familiar with Russian literature?"

Russian! I'd heard there was a small Russian community in Hillbrow. Hillbrovniks, people called them, habitues of Hillbrow's Café Zurich, renowned for its Black Forest torte and strong coffee.

To my surprise, he suddenly began to glow, becoming rainbow-hued, his features distinctively chiseled, and I could see him breathing, his form expanding and contracting with a wavelike rhythm. Blinking rapidly in an effort to restore his sober conventionality, shaking my head as though to clear it of this sudden distortion, I replied, "Only some Dostoevsky and Tolstoy so far, though I'm eager to read more."

"Ah, then you have a store of delight in your future." A second hesitation, then: "If you don't mind my asking, if you'll excuse an old man his curiosity, which books by Tolstoy have you read?"

The panorama beyond the escarpment suddenly heaved, rolling back like a giant tidal wave gathering force before crashing on the shoreline. It gathered the huge hotel/shopping complex of the Carlton Center where the moneyed and the famous wined and dined and where my father, giddy in financial success, also stayed when he came to Jo'burg, and the giant scaffolding rigs of Ponte City, soon to eclipse the Carlton as the tallest building in Africa; it gathered the small unelectrified houses of Soweto, hazy in the dust of unpaved streets, choked by smoke of paraffin and coal fires; it gathered the yellow gold mine waste dumps, their silhouettes blurry from wind blowing over their toxic slopes, gusting particles of uranium, copper, lead, and arsenic to Soweto, coating the township with yellow powder; it gathered the single-sex compounds where mine workers slept on concrete bunkers in dormitories of twenty to fifty; it gathered the mine elevators that took ninety minutes to descend to the rich reserves and ninety minutes to return to the surface. All that lay before us it gathered, from the furthest reaches of the horizon, the deepest depths of the earth, and the highest height of skyscrapers, enfolding everything into the huge arc that surged toward us. I gripped the front edge of the bench, knuckles whitening, the muscles in my arms, back, and neck tensile with terror. As the wave hit the ridge, I ducked, folding my torso over my thighs, screaming.

"Are you in pain?" the old man cried. "Are you unwell? Do you need a doctor?"

Shocked to hear his voice, I realized he was still there on the bench and so was I. We had not been swept away. If I held on to the bench, if I didn't frighten him into leaving, and if he remained beside me, if he would sit and talk, oblivious to the tidal wave I could see in the distance gathering force again, I would be all right. I would be safe.

"I'm not ill," I said, "and I'm not in pain. Some medicine has affected me. It will pass soon. Thank you for asking."

A feeling of immense gratitude, even love, for this stranger, for the gift of his company, his solid shoes, his weary back, his accent, his formality, the tobacco smell of his jacket that filled my nostrils, his old-world fastidiousness, his mustache, filled my heart and dislodged my terror. I wanted to hug and hold on to him, but I knew that would drive him away.

"*War and Peace* and *Anna Karenina*," I answered, pronouncing the latter as *Karaneena*, the way an English-speaker who'd never heard it pronounced by a Russian, would say it.

"Ka-rinnn-nyih-nah" he corrected me, his voice melodic, lingering over the sounds, his pleasure at them moving into the space between and around us.

"Try it," he said, "try to say it like a Russian. It's a beautiful name. In English it is hard."

The wave was almost upon us, not as towering as before, but formidable. Still gripping the bench but turning my face to my companion, focusing on him, though his form had become oddly mutable, I tried sounding the name as he had. He laughed, corrected me, and I, laughing too, tried again. He seemed content to sit beside me that late autumn afternoon on a narrow strip of green in Hillbrow. Perhaps like me he'd left his flat to escape a loneliness not even books could assuage.

Girlhood to Young Adulthood

He spoke of "Mother Russia"—of his childhood in St. Petersburg and of his tutors and studies at the university. He was clearly homesick. Was homesickness infectious? The Swiss doctor Johannes Hofer who coined the word "nostalgia" in 1688 as a diagnostic label for displaced persons, believed it was. I felt homesick too, but why, if I was still in my native country and my native country was a place I longed to leave, would I feel homesick? Or was what I felt melancholia? Freud described melancholia as a refusal to relinquish a lost world, a kind of open wound with the past, a longing for an object not actually dead, but lost as an object of love. I could understand my companion's melancholia, but not my own.

I have no idea how long we sat, though it was long enough for the tidal wave to dissipate and become a series of gentle ripples lapping at our feet—receding, lapping, receding, lapping. I relaxed my grip on the bench. The air grew cold, and my companion grew silent, but still we sat, like two old friends with no need to speak. After a while he looked at his watch, peering at the dial in the darkness, weariness seeming again to settle on him. Endeavoring to heave himself off the bench, not quite succeeding, he spoke again.

"I've been remiss in not mentioning another great Russian writer whose work I would especially like to recommend: Vladimir Nabokov."

"I've always wanted to read *Lolita*," I said, "but it's banned here. Our censors think it will corrupt us."

He sighed heavily, relinquishing his effort to rise, resigning his back to the bench.

"All countries have their problems. We leave our country because we think the problems are too great to bear and then spend the rest of our life longing to return. *Lolita* is a great book, but if you'll excuse an old man's boldness, the Nabokov for you is *Speak, Memory*. Read it sooner rather than later."

I thanked him for the recommendation and promised I would

read it soon. Silence settled on us again. I thought about his reference to "Mother Russia," how impossible the phrase "Mother South Africa" was, and how I couldn't imagine ever longing to return to a country I'd never felt I belonged to.

Then, tipping his weight forward, he rose, turned to retrieve his handkerchief, shook it out, folded it into a neat square, and placed it back in his pocket.

"Thank you for listening to an old man speak about a dead past."

"It lives in you," I said. "I'm grateful you sat beside me."

We shook hands, still without introducing ourselves, and he left slowly the way he'd come. I retraced my steps up the spotless stairwell to my flat.

I wondered which part had been the epiphany. Or had I not had an epiphany at all? Was I, perhaps, not the sort of person to have epiphanies? No matter; I still had two caps in my freezer, two more opportunities. I opened the freezer door, removed the plastic bag and the foil-wrapped caps, unwrapped them, and stared at them, letting the experience of the day wash over me. Then I walked into the bathroom, dropped them into the toilet bowl, held the lever down, and watched the water swirl them around and suck them away. No need to be greedy. If I'd had an epiphany, I had no need of another. And if I hadn't? Well, I wasn't sure I was up for one.

I would read *Speak, Memory* later. *Lolita* too. He was right, my erstwhile companion: *Speak, Memory* is the Nabokov for me. I've returned to it many times, always awed by Nabokov's genius, always reading it slowly—the only way to read Nabokov—for his prose must be savored. Each time I've hoped to absorb a little more of his skill—his ability to capture how incurable is the emigrant's deracination, how fugitive is memory, how unreliable, how confounded, illuminated, and informed by the writer's ability to shift from memory to fiction.

Indiscretion

Two years after we met, H and I married. Given that our courtship and engagement were far from blissful and that I was often unhappy, I should not have married him. But sometimes I *was* happy, or thought I was, and, besides, my parents—especially my father—welcomed him as a son and friend and was thrilled to have a highly credentialed marketing expert with whom to discuss Man About Town; and so I, trusting my father's judgment more than my own, repressed my anxieties about the union. For her part, my mother, repeating to her friends that H was "from a good family," had been tireless in reminding me that I was in danger of becoming "an old maid" because no one had yet asked me to marry them whereas she, at my age (twenty-one) had had seven proposals. I don't blame my parents for my mistake. I blame myself—for not trusting myself enough, for my need to please my parents, and for my own lack of self-worth, which left me vulnerable to other people's ideas for me; and, as it turned out, vulnerable to my father's imprudent love and trust of H; for he shared a secret with him, the revelation of which would have dire consequences for me, not my father.

It happened one late summer weekend in 1975 when H and I had driven eight hours from Johannesburg to visit my parents. My father, impatient, had been watching and waiting for us. At last, observing our car ascend the driveway, he came out to give welcoming hugs. I recall my feeling that it was my husband he was happiest to see.

It was a glorious day. Hot, of course, but late afternoons almost always brought a soft breeze into my mother's garden. It sighed away the turgid humid air, trembled the red bougainvillea blossoms, stirred the dark Dipladenia leaves, breathed gently on the pink hibiscus, and wafted across the pool through the open French doors into the long living room to shimmer over the bar's burnished surface on which my father had set two crystal cut highball glasses.

My father loved being behind that bar—for the pleasure of extending hospitality and for the view across his property. He never tired of that view, never stopped needing its confirmation that he owned this house, this garden, this pool, this grand approach up a long driveway. That view reminded him that he no longer fit his self-description: *I'm just a poor boy from the country, a simple man with simple tastes*—though he still recited the old mantra because, I think, he enjoyed its rags-to-riches plotline and his listener's puzzled effort to reconcile its deprecatory self-description with the successful urbane sophisticate who'd uttered it.

When the house was filled with guests and summer's heat especially oppressive, he'd be behind the bar opening a chilled Chenin Blanc—crisp, flinty, redolent of ripe melons and Cape summers. But as the days shortened and early evenings cooled enough for a long-sleeved shirt or a light sweater, he'd reach for a red, a Cape Pinotage, a wine so deeply red it was almost purple—rustic, earthy and big-flavored. Fumbling, his fingers arthritic, though he was in his fifties and too young for such debilitating arthritis, he'd clumsily open the bottle and pour generously. Though he knew better and even fancied himself a wine maven, he was usually too eager or too lusty or too thirsty to let aromas of smoky tobacco and ripe strawberry bloom, too impatient to hold the glass to the light to admire its inky hue. The wine poured, he'd edge the too-full glasses across the bar to his guests, spilling, laughing at his eager clumsiness. Raising his glass by the bowl, not the stem, he'd drink deeply, grimacing at the sharp tannins, relishing the first heady flush as alcohol dilated his pores.

It was a while before H and I could join him at the bar, for my mother, excited to have her daughter home, ushered us to my old bedroom—our accommodation for the weekend—fussing lovingly before we excused ourselves to take showers.

At last, we joined him. Impatient, his cup running over, he'd already filled the two waiting glasses. A smoky fragrance of whisky filled the air. That day his drink of choice was scotch. A drink for men. A drink to celebrate a weekend with his son-in-law. H drew up a barstool on the bar's convex side opposite my father, who stood within the bar's concave embrace. I perched on a stool outside the radius of their rapport, content to be peripheral, happy that the two most significant men in my life were keen to build on their mutual affection.

"Good to have you in the family," my father said to H.

"Good to be in the family," H replied.

Their glasses emptied, my father refilled them. Resting his forearms on the bar, his chronically tight shoulders visibly softening, he leaned toward H, into the zone of intimacy.

"Family's everything," he said, "and because you're family now, I'll tell you something strictly confidential. Not to go beyond this room. Strictly a matter for this family."

I had no idea what confidential information my father was about to share. My husband and father had entered man-to-man territory; and I, on the outer edge of their affinity, had become invisible.

Their eyes locked. Then, as if on cue to seal a pact, they raised their glasses, arched back their necks, drained the elixir, and, in unison, set down their emptied vessels.

I watched the whisky tears, legs of caramel gold, trail slowly down the etched walls of crystal.

Expectation hung over the bar—my husband's at the promise of a secret, my father's at the pleasure of the story he was about to tell. My father let the expectation linger. He was a skilled orator, attuned to the power of the pregnant pause. His was a natural talent, honed, like all natural talent, by diligent practice. Often in my childhood I'd seen him pace up and down the hallway in front of the tall gilt mirror practicing the delivery of a speech, trying out cadence, timing, and vocabulary, gauging for maximum effect. That late summer as he launched slowly and deliberately into the sharing of a secret, I knew he'd rehearsed it.

His story began with a trip to Germany to buy cloth for the

factory. The trip was mainly business but not only business, for Sadie came with him, and they took a few days here and there to vacation. They went to Zurich for the fine dining, though personally he preferred peasant food, a simple man with simple tastes, but the lake view was great, worth the cost of admission; and also for the museums because Sadie, as you know, loves art, especially Picasso, and there was a big show on. This part was mainly pleasure, mainly holiday, but not entirely, for he'd scheduled a meeting with the manager of the Credit Suisse Bank. The purpose of the meeting? To open an account and to inquire about getting money out of South Africa.

Ah, here was the secret, the revelation of which could send my father to jail. The apartheid government pursued and prosecuted anyone who contravened South Africa's stringent security exchange regulations, for the rand was in crisis. Western countries were boycotting us, and the government was determined to halt the exodus of money.

"What I wanted to know, what I asked the bank manager," my father told my husband, "was: did the bank, for a fee—of course—offer a courier service? I need to get money out, and I can't do it personally because it's too risky to pack rands or dollars into luggage. I've heard, via the grapevine, that you're set up to help."

He had my husband's full attention.

"The bank manager told me it wasn't legal for a major prominent bank like his to do that sort of thing. But they had a subsidiary, a satellite bank that handled that sort of transaction, and they could arrange a connection and put me in touch with an agent who would take care of the whole thing. For a fee, of course."

He paused. He'd waited a long time for someone to tell this story to, someone he could trust, and he wasn't about to rush it.

"How did you know you could trust the agent?" H asked.

"I didn't. I had to take him on faith. It was a risk." He chuckled. I'd never thought of my father as a risk taker.

"The connection at the satellite bank told me I'd get a call after

I returned to South Africa. The call would come late at night. The caller would be the courier. He'd say, 'The man from Milan is here.'"

The code was ridiculous. If I hadn't known my father so well, I'd have suspected he was having my husband on. But my father was not an imaginative man. Though he read fiction in his youth, as an adult he abjured it. I'd once seen a John le Carré novel on our bookshelf, and when I asked him about it, he told me someone had left it at the house; *he* never read that sort of rubbish. That was as close as he ever got to spy novels. His passion was exclusively political biography. He never could have made up a story about some mysterious man from Milan. It wasn't in the lexicon of his imagination.

"The connection told me the caller, the courier, would give me a pick-up time for the next Saturday afternoon. I was to have the money ready in an attaché and watch out for him. He would drive by the house once and then circle back and come up the driveway and take the attaché from me. Forty-eight hours later, I'd get another call to let me know the money had been deposited. The caller would say, 'The man from Milan has returned,' and I'd know my money was safe in Zurich in my account at Credit Suisse. Minus the fee, of course."

H, usually quick to comment, said nothing. I couldn't gauge his thoughts.

"I got the call," my father continued. "I had the money ready, and about an hour before the appointed time on the appointed Saturday I started watching for the courier. I stood *there*," he gestured at the garden, "and waited. At last, a black car drove slowly by. *Slowwwly.* Much more slowly than regular traffic. It drove past and I began to worry. But it came back and came up the driveway and a man got out and I handed him the attaché. Neither of us said a word. Forty-eight hours later I got the call: 'The man from Milan has returned.' My money was safe."

As though on cue, as though she'd been waiting for my father to finish his story, my mother, who'd been supervising the servants in the kitchen, called us to dinner. My father grabbed a bottle of Pinotage, and we joined my brothers and sister in the dining room.

H and I never spoke of what we'd heard. I'm not sure he registered that I was there. I think I was invisible to him and my father—just a girl on the outer edge of serious talk between men. But if what my father later told me was true, he remembered the story. Years later, he pulled it out.

On June 16, 1976, South Africa once again erupted in political violence—arguably the most serious since the apartheid regime assumed power in 1948. The trigger was a 1974 government directive, the Afrikaans Medium Decree, about the language of instruction for African schoolchildren: Afrikaans was to be the medium of instruction for mathematics, arithmetic, and social studies; English for homecraft, needlework, woodwork, metalwork, art, and agricultural science; indigenous languages would be used only for religious instruction, music, and physical culture. The ruling, intended to reverse the decline of Afrikaans among Black Africans, backfired: Africans deeply resented a mandate to study the sciences in the language of the oppressors; having to do so would cause them to focus on the language instead of the subject.

On the morning of June 16 a crowd of between 3,000 and 10,000 Black students marched from their schools to Orlando Stadium singing and waving placards with slogans like "Down with Afrikaans," "Viva Azania," and "If we must do Afrikaans, Vorster [the prime minister] must do Zulu." Police fired into the crowd, killing twenty-three children. There were other collateral casualties, like Melville Edelstein, the son of Lithuanian Jews who had emigrated to South Africa in 1896, a few years after my grandfather Joseph. Melville, a sociologist, academic, and practicing Orthodox Jew, had devoted his life to humanitarian and social welfare projects in Soweto. Attempting to rescue a female colleague, he was stoned to death by a crowd of enraged students. His body was found with a note: "Beware: Afrikaans is the most dangerous drug for our future." Edelstein, an ardent opponent of the racist regime, was not Afrikaans.

The revolution, it seemed, was at hand. The uprising spread across the country; underground sabotage actions against the government intensified; trained guerilla fighters armed with Soviet and Eastern bloc weapons infiltrated the country; there were bombings. In response, the government became even more repressive, but nothing could now contain the rising tide of antigovernment fervor. Additionally, countries joined forces in boycotting South Africa, and the rand began its precipitous fall.

Whites panicked. It was time to leave.

My sister had already left; my father made plans to sell his business and the family home and move his dependents; H, who had contacts in the United States and a prestigious business credential, was hired by a major multinational California company; my brother Michael, completing his economics degree at Wits, would leave as soon as he graduated.

5

Leaving

H AND I DEPARTED ON JUNE 22, 1977. WE HAD ONE-WAY TICKETS to California. My parents, who would soon leave on one-way tickets to Israel, were at Jan Smuts Airport to see us off. I thought my father would be happy I was leaving, but he seemed unable to let me disappear down the on-ramp to the plane.

"Just one more hug," he said.

"For God's sake, Jo-Anne. Get a move on," my husband called from the departures gate.

"Wait, Joey," said my father. "I want to give you something."

Fumbling in his pocket, searching, he pulled out a small flat object and pressed it into my palm.

"A silly thing," he said, "for good luck."

"I'll keep it forever," I said, not knowing what he'd given me and too hurried to look lest the doors close before I could join H.

Belted into my seat, flying over Johannesburg, I stared out the window, surprised to find myself in conflict about leaving. I'd identified with Jo'burg in ways I never had with Durban. I'd become an adult there, made friendships, acquired a profession, become a married woman with a house and a garden and a pool, and I was leaving it all. My husband, seemingly intent on *The Wall Street Journal*, cast no fond looks through the window. But his situation, I told myself, was different. He'd been a graduate student in Berkeley's MBA program, had worked in San Francisco for a year after graduating, and had friends and memories that connected him to the Golden State. I'd spent a total of four days there when I'd accompanied H on his job interview trip and knew no one. But I'd been accepted into Stanford's art history graduate program. I reminded myself that I had much to anticipate.

I realized I was sweating. My left fist was clenched. My left arm was taut. I was clutching something. The object from my father! I uncurled my fist. It was a coin, a twenty-cent piece. I stared at it. I'd handled dozens, maybe hundreds like it, but had never before *looked* at one. Now I did.

On its front face was a portrait of Jan van Riebeeck; on the reverse was a picture of a springbok, South Africa's national animal, and the date the coin was minted: 1961. It struck me that the two sides bookended a South African narrative that spanned three hundred years. The narrative began with van Riebeeck's arrival at the Cape of Good Hope on April 6, 1652, to establish a refreshment station for Dutch ships carrying slaves and spices to and from the East. Van Riebeeck's employer, the Dutch East India Company, never intended to start a colony, but van Riebeeck's settlement became one, and the colony became a country, and South Africa honored van Riebeeck as its founding father and the date of his arrival as a national holiday.

It was a history I hadn't identified with and didn't want. But I was born into it. My birthday is April 7, the day after the day honoring van Riebeeck. All these decades later, 11,000 miles from South Africa, I always, inadvertently, remember van Riebeeck on the eve of my birthday.

The coin's reverse side, the side with the springbok and the date, carried a different set of baggage: in 1961, I was eleven years old and aware that I lived in a troubled land.

Staring at the coin, *looking* at it, the art historian in me kicked in, distancing and distracting me from a history I was ashamed of. With the dispassionate curiosity a scholar brings to a strange artifact, I examined the picture of van Riebeeck for iconography and style. The image was, I knew, based on a portrait of van Riebeeck in the Rijksmuseum and was, like Grandpa's Vermeer, a product of the Golden Age of Dutch Art—the same period that had brought van Riebeeck to the Cape.

The face on the coin, like the face of the original, was European, handsome, aristocratic, and worldly; the brow was noble, the gaze clear and direct, the mouth full-lipped and soft; the not quite shoulder-length hair signified membership in a social class that did not labor; the somber jacket with its delicate trim—refined, restrained, expensive—spoke of seemly Calvinist moderation. It was the face of a man from the seventeenth century's richest and most sophisticated culture, who had brought European culture's "light" to Africa, who'd planted a garden and cultivated grapes for wine. It was a beautiful face, a face behind which a nation might rally and take pride; a face a nation might deploy, emblematically, on its currency.

Years later I would learn that the face on the coin was not van Riebeeck's. The Rijks had made an error. The South African government and the South African mint, searching for an iconic image to replace Queen Elizabeth when we broke from the Commonwealth, as yet unaware of the Rijks's error, adopted the mistake. At some point

Leaving 131

Portrait of a Man, probably Bartholomeus Vermuyden (1616/17—1650), Dirck Craey, Rijksmuseum, Amsterdam.

in the early 1980s, the portrait was reidentified as Bartholomeus Vermuyden, a man who almost certainly never set foot in the Cape Colony and was innocent of the iniquities inflicted by van Riebeeck on the Khoisan.

The Rijks would, in 1984, identify another image as van Riebeeck, a painting by a second-rate artist identified only as "anon" and dated to 1662.

The figure is bulky, its mass defined more by displacement of space and linear outline than by proficiency in modeling. The face—round, puffy, pudgy—is weary. Behind the figure a red, gold-trimmed curtain parts to reveal the ocean, an odd flat-topped mountain, and an island: Table Bay, Table Mountain, and Robben Island—geographical markers that identify the Cape Colony and van Riebeeck.

By the time I would learn of the misidentification, South Africa would have moved on. Apartheid would be over. No one in the new South Africa would care whose face had been on our currency. I

Portrait of Jan van Riebeeck, anon, Rijksmuseum, Amsterdam.

would care. I would want to know what it meant—that the face of our currency through all the years of apartheid, the face we were taught to revere as the face of the country's founding father, was not the founding father's, not van Riebeeck's. What, I would wonder, did it mean that a borrowed face, a false face, had been on our national currency? Would our government's self-conception have been any different had a face more weary and less noble represented us?

The misidentification would give me a kind of sour pleasure, a sense of poetic justice that the face South Africa presented to the world was a mistake. The mistake captured for me the apartheid government's utter craziness in claiming simultaneously to be furthering the West's "enlightenment" enterprise while embarking on policies that ran counter to that enterprise.

I would break my promise to my father, for I would lose the coin, and its loss would distress me, and I would search for it frantically until I finally accepted that it was gone. I had thought to have it forever, for upon arrival in California I had a locksmith drill a hole into it so I could thread a key ring through it to hold the keys to the doors I would open in my new life in America—though now I think it odd to have wanted to keep the image of van Riebeeck with me. By the time I lost it I would have caressed it so often with my thumb and forefinger that I wore down the images so they became barely recognizable, though it would take many more years to understand that I could never rub away the history sandwiched between the coin's two sides because that history is my history, though I still wish it were not.

From the coin in my palm, I turned to my husband. I wanted to connect with him, to hold his hand and have him hold mine, to talk with him about a new life in which the face on our currency would be George Washington—a face without baggage in our personal histories. But he was reading, hunched over the folded-down drinks tray on which he'd spread *The Wall Street Journal.* Surely he'd noticed I'd turned to him? But he did not look up. He had shut me out.

This was not new. Our relationship had been punctuated by his withdrawals, and I still struggled to understand what triggered them. Now, seated beside him, I tried to recall my impressions when I'd first met him: he was exotic and funny and irreverent and playful. Six years later, tied to each other in what felt like a suffocating coil, those adjectives no longer applied. What had happened? When had it happened? In my liminal state—in flight between countries, suspended betwixt my past and my future, deracinated—I tried to take stock of my marriage—and myself.

For some time, I'd been troubled by a nagging question: had I viewed H as my ticket out of South Africa? I cringed at the thought, but the truth was that with his Berkeley MBA and extensive business experience, he was exportable and marketable in ways that I, with only honors degrees in English literature and art history, was not. From that perspective, H *was* my ticket, for I would, through him, receive a green card when we arrived at San Francisco International.

Had I hung on to him for that green ticket? I didn't think so; I hoped not. I didn't think I was that calculating. But why had I stayed in the unhappy marriage? What had kept us together? Seated beside him on the plane, the question would not stop gnawing at me.

And then I remembered something I'd not yet had time to process:

A few days before our departure, when I was packing up our house for shipment to California, I'd come across letters he'd written to me both before and after we married. He'd written them when I was away in Durban visiting my parents. And in that moment, seated on the plane and remembering when I'd come across his letters and held them in my hands, I became two people: a woman flying toward her future in California and a woman in the Johannesburg house she would soon leave forever. I saw that young woman, large packing boxes all around her, in her hands a stash of letters from H; saw her stare at the little stash, deliberating whether to read or not to read; and then I saw her cross her ankles and sit down on the floor and read.

Alone in that unhappy house, rereading letters she'd only ever read in her brief separations from her husband, the young woman saw a pattern she'd not previously noticed: each letter began with a paragraph of affirmations—*protestations* is probably a better word—of H's love for her. The second paragraph was an apology: for having spoken harshly to her, for having made her cry, for having shut her out. The third and following paragraphs gave reasons for his behavior: he was unhappy at work; he hated his bachelor uncle; he'd been having acute diarrhea; he was confused about his career path; he was depressed, introspective, self-involved, irritable, on a bad trip, detached, uninvolved, antisocial, unable to get out of bed to go to work. In the last paragraph of every letter, he wrote that he loved and needed her and longed for her return. It was that last paragraph that always reeled her back in.

A young wife, troubled, unsure of her marriage, cross-legged on the floor. Amid the disorder of boxes she sat, inhaling the dust of a troubled marriage. For a long while she remained on the floor, her husband's letters in her lap, her gaze as unfocused as her future. At last, coming to, she refolded the letters and replaced them in the box from which she'd removed them.

Her mouth was set. She'd surely learned *something*, though she wasn't sure what. Now on the plane she/I did: They were all the same letter. There was a pattern: She/I was a yo-yo on a string and he was the yo-yo master, spinning her out, reeling her in; and when she was out, she was lost and sad and self-accusing and self-doubting; and when he reeled her back in, she'd forget the oscillation of the yo-yo: out and in, out and in; forgetting, she'd nestle into the relief of being drawn back in.

I was startled out of my reverie, drawn back to my present—beside my husband, on the plane—by a pretty flight attendant with a drinks wagon in the aisle beside my husband.

"What would you like to drink?"

Instantly attentive, instantly charming, quick with banter, H ordered a gin and tonic and joked about it being a colonial cocktail. I waited for him to ask if I would like a drink, but he turned from the attendant back to *The Wall Street Journal*, took a sip of his cocktail, crossed his legs, and shifted his torso toward the aisle and away from me. The attendant looked inquiringly at me. I'd have loved a glass of wine with the pretzel nibbles she'd just handed us, something bracing and acidic to offset their oily saltiness. I hesitated, then declined. I was not disposed to drink alone.

PART 2:
NEW WORLD, NEW LIFE

6

California

CALIFORNIA UNDER OUR FEET, OUR GREEN CARDS IN HAND, WE embarked on our new lives. Motel 6 was "home" until we found a house to rent: a little bungalow with a small backyard on Cowper Street in Palo Alto. I was, at first, enchanted by the house, but as days and weeks went by it seemed to absorb our troubles and lose its luster. I noticed that the door handles and drawer pulls were fragile, wobbly, and rusted; that old grime had caked into the tile grout, and that the walls—thin and damp—felt more menacing than protective. I seemed to see behind their fragile surface spores of mold multiplying and spreading mephitic vapors into our emotionally toxic air. Even the little yard seemed hostile. I longed to sink down roots—to grow vegetables, herbs, and flowers—but there wasn't enough sunshine. Mornings, the tall thick hedge cast dark shade; afternoons, it was the shadow of the house that made the garden cold and gloomy.

When our possessions were delivered in a U-Haul, I greeted them like long-lost friends, tenderly unwrapping each item of crockery and cutlery, nesting them into their new home, though most of my beloved books I had to store, still in boxes, in the garage. But contrary to my hopes, H and I could not nest. Though we shared a bed, we were tense roommates, more tense even than in South Africa, each at ease only in the other's absence.

Not ready to surrender my dream of home, I turned to cooking. Making beautiful meals gave me pleasure. My passion for cooking had been triggered by a wedding gift from my friend Zoe: a boxed set of Elizabeth David's five "handbooks" to the cooking of France and Italy. David, the beloved doyen of English cookery, had cast sunshine into Britain's postwar gloom with her promise of Mediterranean warmth: picnics of fish terrines, salads fragrant with herbs, and platters of figs with fresh cheese, all washed down with unpretentious wine in the company of friends, preferably in the country under a leafy bower. Elizabeth David was a consummate prose writer: syntactically perfect, precise, elegant, and able to capture the allure of France and Italy. I relished her books as much for her essays and reflections as for her recipes. That boxed set was the start of my fascination with cooking and food history and of a personal cookbook library that would, at times, easily top five hundred volumes. On the day I unpacked my goods into our Palo Alto home, that future culinary library consisted only of Elizabeth David. She was treasure enough. I embraced the five-volume set, ecstatic at our reunion.

Those books fed my fantasy of a home filled with the aromas of delicious food, home as a beacon of hospitality, home as a refuge of nurturance. Like Britons in the 1950s and '60s, I turned to Elizabeth David to lift me out of despondency. But there was no point cooking. H, in love with American fast food, came home each evening with something in a box to consume behind a closed door in the room he'd claimed as his "office." Exiled and alone, I supped on imagined feasts.

We arrived in June. H started work almost immediately, but my fall quarter at Stanford would not begin until September. I had time to acculturate, time to overcome my terror of entering and exiting freeways—a challenge compounded by the vehicle H had purchased for me: a used Pontiac Grand Ville. In Johannesburg I'd driven a VW Beetle, a darling little blue bug. The Pontiac was a behemoth, its front end so long I couldn't, from the driver's seat, tell where it ended; parallel parking was an ordeal, reverse parking impossible. The scale of the vehicle and everything else in this new world was overwhelmingly huge, the tempo impossibly fast. I felt dizzy, desperate for a way to shrink immensity into a frame I could manage.

I found solace in my studies. Scholarly engagement had always centered me, easing anxiety by giving me something to focus on that wasn't me. Stanford was waiting; I had a place to go and a career to pursue. Successfully maneuvering the Grand Ville monster into a roomy parking bay under an oak tree, I set off across the bucolic Stanford campus in search of the art department. The office staff gave me a warm welcome, a tour, and a carrel in the library. That carrel, my own personal study space, became the harbor from which I ventured to explore the rich underground stacks.

On my floor was American art, the history of which, prior to Abstract Expressionism, I knew very little. Here was my opportunity: I would root myself in my adoptive country by studying American art. On the narrow shelf of my carrel I piled a tower of books. I began with the colonial period, moved on to landscape painting, and found myself fixated on a painting by Thomas Cole, founder of the American landscape tradition and of what came to be called the Hudson River School.

Cole's painting *The Oxbow, a View from Mt. Holyoke after a Storm*, 1836, shows a glorious landscape punctuated by a river that doubles back on itself like a question mark. Cole exaggerated the river's loop to make it *more* like a question mark; other renderings of the site show it less so. The distant view is arcadian, but dark storm clouds gather on the far left. In the foreground, the artist, barely visible, is at his easel painting the scene we see. He turns to the viewer as if to ask: Is this a promised land or one doomed? Cole's question was about the morality of westward expansion, but I took it personally;

the gathering storm clouds on the left were part of my own sense of foreboding, the sunshine on the right met my need for hope.

The Oxbow, a View from Mount Holyoke After a Storm, 1836, Thomas Cole, Metropolitan Museum of Art, New York.

Every day I took myself to the library, to that small slice of the world beneath the stacks I'd claimed as mine; but something was happening to me that I couldn't understand: Each morning as I settled in, I was overcome by unaccustomed fatigue. Heedless of the books perched on my carrel's narrow shelf, I'd fold my arms, lay my head down, and sleep, grateful that my floor had so little traffic. My unusual fatigue troubled me enough that I consulted a doctor. I learned I was pregnant.

Looking back, I easily identified the date conception had occurred. There was only one possibility: the night before movers descended on our house to pack it up for shipment to California. Overwhelmed by the huge changes we'd initiated, H and I had clung to each other and made love. Months earlier I'd stopped taking birth control pills; stress and low body weight had caused my periods to stop and there'd seemed no need for contraception. We hadn't planned on a baby, but I welcomed the news. Perhaps the baby would be our sunshine after the storm.

I'd been accepted into Stanford on the strength of my honors thesis: an examination of the relationship of Henry VIII and Hans Holbein the Younger. Shortly after my acceptance by Stanford and my response that I would be thrilled to come, I received a warm personal note from the senior medievalist on the faculty: She'd found my work interesting and insightful and looked forward to working with me; she would be away until a few days before the start of the fall quarter and hoped I would seek her out before classes commenced. At the appropriate time I made an appointment.

Her office door was open. I announced myself. She looked up from a book and examined me before gesturing to the chair opposite her desk. I stepped over a small pile of books to get to it, causing papers to flutter to the floor. Apologetically, I tried to restore them, but she, impatient, commanded me to sit. She was probably twenty years older than I; lean, middle-aged, with steel-gray hair pulled into a bun, her gray eyes framed by steel-rimmed spectacles. Jewelry mitigated her severity: the hand that had gestured me to sit bore on its central digit an ornate ring with a large black onyx; from a chain around her neck hung an exquisite pendant with garnets and pearls in filigree roundels. Reposing on the breastbone of her dusty pink shirt with its ruffled collar, the delicate pendant, like the collar, seemed to gesture at femininity, signs, perhaps, that within the wearer's breast there raged an unresolved war between the severe and the soft.

Her office had the kind of disorder that suggests creative research: books and papers everywhere, large metal files half open, a fine film of dust overlaying all. Perhaps, I thought, she likes dust; perhaps it reminds her of time's passage, of her calling as an historian of a time long past. Charmed and intrigued, I was ready to accept her as my mentor, as my scholarly mother who would induct me into the mysteries of the American academy. But as her silent examination of me continued, I began to feel uncomfortable, uncertain where to rest my eyes. I longed to focus on the striking ring and pendant, but that seemed impertinent, and so I looked into my lap, over the almost imperceptible swell of my growing belly. After her warm letter, I'd anticipated an enthusiastic welcome. I badly needed one.

"Are you pregnant?" she asked.

Clearly, I was showing more than I'd thought. Or perhaps her eye, accustomed to medieval representations of the pregnant Virgin, tender Madonnas of Parturition, was sensitized to the sight of a slight protuberance in the lower belly.

"Yes. It was a surprise. I'm into my second trimester."

"You'll need to make a decision, Jo-Anne. You can't do both. You can't be a mother and a scholar. It doesn't work. I speak from experience. You'll need to figure it out and come to a decision."

I remember the moment vividly. A punch to the solar plexus. An instant of shock and stupefaction. What I don't remember is what came after, what I said to her, how I left her office, or where I went. What I know is that I resolved never to take a class from her. I would not become a medievalist. I became a modernist.

First Thanksgiving

Fall came, and with it my first experience of American holidays. Determined to integrate, longing to belong, I carved a jack-o-lantern and bought candy for children. The next holiday—as unfamiliar to a South African as Halloween or Presidents' Day—was Thanksgiving—another opportunity to embrace my new American identity.

My husband approached me with a proposal. Here's how it happened:

The last couple of weeks had been a surprise, for he'd been pleasant, even friendly. Ah, I thought, California is working its magic.

He's happier away from the toxicity of South Africa, more like the man I met and fell in love with six years before. Gone—forgotten or repressed—was the memory of sitting on the floor and rereading his letters; gone, forgotten, or repressed was my understanding on the plane that he'd played me like a yo-yo. All I knew, weeks into our new life in California, was the possibility—now that he was reaching out to me—of a connected future.

A few days into this state of restored connection, he took me to a Mexican restaurant for dinner. I was happy we would be eating together instead of he, alone, in his "office," and I, alone, at an imagined Elizabeth David feast with imagined guests. I ordered a fish taco; he ordered a burrito; we shared a guacamole dip; he drank a beer and became expansive; he drank a second and became maudlin. He began to cry. His job, he said, was overwhelming; there were so many people whose names he had to remember, so many people he had to impress; the hierarchy of management was rigid; everyone was organized, serious, and efficient; every day he received stacks of reports to study; every day he received assignments of reports he had to write; he felt like a foreigner; he had diarrhea; he was uptight and anxious and doubted he could survive in a business world so different from the family business in South Africa where the only person with more status than he was his difficult uncle. He needed me, he said, to understand, to be kind, to be tolerant, to help him through this.

I wasn't sure how to respond. I wanted to comfort him, to put my arms around him, but for weeks he'd operated from behind a barrier. Though we were now together at a restaurant, a married couple on a date, I still felt the barrier—barrier*s*—mine as much as his, for I'd withdrawn in reaction to his withdrawal. It would take effort and courage to reach through our self-enclosures and touch. Watching him cry was odd. I'd always been the weepy one, and he'd always dismissed my weepiness as manipulation. Now I wondered if he was manipulating me. The thought was unkind, and I felt remorse for entertaining it. I moved my hand across the table to touch his, but he reached for a paper napkin and wiped his eyes. I let my hand rest at the place his had been. I wanted to tell him I wished he'd shared his suffering sooner because I'd felt so shut out, and that had caused me to suffer; but I knew he'd take it as a reproach. I felt I was damned if I reached out and damned if I didn't, that whatever I did or didn't do would become the next issue between us. But I had to say or do something.

"I'm sorry you're going through this," I said. "Of course I'm here for you. And yes, it's difficult, but we're in it together. You can count on me. I'll do whatever I can to help. All you need do is tell me what you need."

He lowered his hand from his face and relinquished the napkin. I covered his hand with mine—lightly, for his sake and mine.

"We're from the arsehole of the world," he said. "I don't want to go back to it, but I don't know if I can survive here. If I can't, I doubt you can."

His comment upset me. I wanted to remove my hand. I had as many reservations about South Africa as he, but I hated his visceral description of the country—one he resorted to often— and always found myself, when he did, wanting to defend it; at the very least, to take issue with the crudeness of his characterization. But this was not the moment to discuss metonymy. And I was hurt by his lack of confidence, his belief that I would not "survive" in America. I wanted to remove my hand, but I left it there, though even more lightly now, reluctant and out of place.

"I'll be OK," I said, not knowing if that were true, but determined, now that he'd expressed his doubt, to prove him wrong. "I'm more resilient and determined than you give me credit for."

Sliding his hand from under mine, he reached for a chip and scooped a glob of guacamole.

"I've been thinking about Thanksgiving," he said. "It's an important American holiday. I think it's a good idea for us to host it, to have people over to our home. You don't know anyone to invite, but I have friends from my Berkeley and commune days. You used to say you'd love to meet them. Do you still want to? Can you manage sixteen?"

"Yes," I said, taken aback though pleased. "I love cooking for company, and I can manage sixteen."

Back on Cowper Street, I reached for my Elizabeth David boxed set and scoured each volume for turkey recipes. There were a few. *French Country Cooking* suggested that "the legs or wings of a turkey go very well in cassoulet," but that didn't seem American. Then there was "Turkey a la Chevaliere," but that was served cold, with mayonnaise. "Salmis de Dinde a la Berrichonne" looked promising, but that was a stew with bacon, mushrooms, and triangles of fried bread and would not do.

I was in pursuit of the magnificent, gargantuan, burnished bird in Norman Rockwell's 1943 painting *Freedom from Want*.

I'd come to know the painting well. The stacks near my carrel held books on Rockwell, and I'd been perusing them. Though I'd studied mid-twentieth-century American art in South Africa, I was familiar only with high art, most notably the Abstract Expressionist movement of the 1940's and '50s and the high-cultural critic Clement Greenberg who'd espoused it. Greenberg had even come to South Africa, bringing his gospel of high modernism to a packed audience of worshippers I'd been part of. I didn't know much of the "lowbrow" world he'd scathingly denigrated in his famous 1939 essay "Avant Garde and Kitsch." He'd not mentioned Rockwell. There'd been no need, for Greenberg damned illustrators, populists, and storytellers as kitsch, and Rockwell fit those bills. But I was interested in broadening my knowledge of pre- and post-WWII American culture, and Rockwell was as much part of that period as Pollock and Greenberg. And so, to the growing pile on my carrel, I added Rockwell.

Contrary to expectations, I was charmed by him. His paintings made me happy. They were wholesome, optimistic, celebrating what it meant to be an American; they were tolerant and forgiving, full of nice people being kind to one another. I wanted that world; I wanted to step into the paintings and never leave; to join the family gathered around the Thanksgiving table with its exquisite still life of grapes, apples, and pears in the foreground, its silver tureen, its dish of golden butter, and the glorious, burnished bird that no one, save the elderly hosts illuminated by the bright window behind them, paid attention to, for the family members were lovingly engaged with one another. I didn't care that Rockwell was sentimental, that the domestic sublime he offered might never have existed. It consoled me. I believed it. I wanted the generous benignity of his world.

I acceded to H's request to host sixteen strangers for lots of reasons. First, I'd told him I would do whatever I could to help him, that all he had to do was ask, and he'd asked. Second, I was curious about the people who'd been his friends when he'd lived in the United States. I *did* want to meet them. Third, I loved cooking projects that demanded new skills, complex menu orchestration, and culinary engagement with an unfamiliar culture—which America and Thanksgiving were. And then there was Rockwell. His Thanksgiving painting fed my fantasy of finding and making Home. I wanted a Rockwellian Thanksgiving, a "freedom from want" in the house on Cowper Street.

Recognizing that I needed more help than Elizabeth David could give me, I turned to the most welcoming people I'd met in the States: the office staff of the Stanford Art Department.

The following day, before heading down to my carrel, I stopped there.

"Do any of you have any tried-and-true family recipes for Thanksgiving that you might be willing to share?" I asked. "It's my first and we're hosting sixteen."

There was a moment of silence and then everyone spoke at once. I tried taking notes but couldn't keep up. Eventually someone said, "Poor thing. We're confusing her. Come back tomorrow. We'll have it all figured out for you—a menu with recipes."

The following day they handed me an envelope with index cards. Grateful, I labeled it "First Thanksgiving, 1977." I pictured it as the start of an archive that would, over the years, grow fat with Thanksgivings. I would fill it with recipes, memories, menus, and names of guests, and every year as the envelope swelled, I would feel myself becoming more American, more at home, less like a transplanted alien.

Days before the big day, Rockwell's tableau imprinted on the register of my desires, I paid a visit to the Williams Sonoma store in the Town and Country Shopping Center. I adored that store; it was a temple for cooks, a repository of hallowed vessels and exalted implements for kitchen and table. I knew I would find everything I needed there.

The sales staff knew me, for I'd wandered the aisles many times, slowly, as though in a dream, wanting to reach out and touch, but restraining myself, for I'd not, hitherto, come to purchase, only to look, as one does in a museum, where, between visitor and object, there obtrudes always an invisible barrier, a yellow tape with the words: *don't touch*. But this day I had come to possess; and I would, brazenly, touch.

"Are you ready for Thanksgiving?" an assistant asked.

"I have what I need to make the meal," I said, "but I need serving implements, a platter, a tureen, a white tablecloth. It's my first Thanksgiving and I'm not yet equipped."

"Do you have a roasting pan?"

"A disposable aluminum one from Safeway."

"Let me show you what we have. Lovely things you'll keep forever and be proud to set out for your guests."

I followed her to a shelf of copper roasting pans.

"They're hand-hammered," she said, "to Chuck Williams's exacting specifications, produced by craftsmen at the Ruffoni workshop in northern Piedmont in the Italian Alps. They're as beautiful as they're functional. They're heirlooms."

A roasting pan had not been on my shopping list, for I'd written down only the accoutrements on Rockwell's table. But now, standing before an object that could not have been part of Rockwell's vision, for in his day there was no Williams Sonoma and no Chuck Williams, I knew at once that, had Rockwell known of this exquisite roasting pan, he would surely have featured it.

I imagined my turkey nestled within it; thyme, rosemary, and sage rubbed into its pearly plumpness; later, roasted, its bronzed skin would surpass Norman Rockwell's peerless example. I imagined the oohs and ahs of my guests. I would be proud to set such a magnificent object— turkey and pan a united whole—on my Thanksgiving table—this year and in years to come.

Still caught in my reverie, I reached out and touched the solid brass handle. The other hand rested on my belly. Yes, an heirloom. I would pass it on to my baby.

"Yes, yes," I murmured. "I'll return the aluminum pan."

My guide led me to another part of the store where, under her approving gaze, I reached out, touched, and took: a white porcelain gravy boat, a white tureen, a flowered Provencal platter for green beans, an embossed butter dish, an orange ruffled pie dish, ceramic pumpkin candleholders, two packages of orange paper napkins that said *Happy Thanksgiving,* and, for cranberry sauce, an amber glass bowl shaped like a resplendent-tailed turkey. I handed over my credit card.

I returned to the house on Cowper Street with my treasures. H would not be home for a couple of hours, time enough to put everything away until their Thanksgiving debut. H would be annoyed at my expenditure, but my precious purchases would so honor our celebration that I was sure that he would overlook my uncharacteristic extravagance.

Early Thanksgiving morning I set the table, adorned its center with a bouquet of yellow, white, and orange daisies, and festooned the room with garlands of paper pumpkins. My herb-rubbed, butter-anointed turkey I nestled into the copper roasting pan atop a bed of root vegetables. Mopping the kitchen floor came next—a task I was new to, a skill I'd acquired only days before leaving South Africa. Every time I mopped, I remembered the scene of my instruction: the kitchen of our Johannesburg house, and the person of my instructor: Rosie, who'd left her job at my Hillbrow apartment building to work for us when I married.

"Rosie," I'd asked, "could you please show me how to mop a floor? I'm going to have to do it myself in America. No one has servants there."

Rosie slapped a hand over her mouth in disbelief. No servants! What a strange country! She filled a bucket with water, showed me how to hold a mop, and my lesson began.

H, passing the open kitchen door, had paused, amused at the sight of a white woman supervised by her Black domestic worker.

"Why don't you come with us, Rosie?" he said. "You should come with us, you and Petrus and your boys. Come to America."

"Thank you, Master," she said, "I speak with Petrus. I speak tonight with Petrus."

"You do that," he said. "You ask him. You should come with us."

After she left, I turned on him with unaccustomed fury.

"How could you say that to her! You know we can't take her. Of course they'll want to come. Of course they want a better future for their boys. How could you let her think we could possibly take them!"

"For fuck's sake, lighten up, Jo-Anne. It was a joke. She knew I was joking."

The following morning, when I greeted Rosie, she said, "I good news. Petrus, he say: Yes. Yes, we come with you to America."

I had to tell her H had been joking.

The floor was mopped; the house was clean; the turkey was in the oven; I was ready. Guests began arriving. H emerged from the second bedroom where he'd been all day behind a closed door. Now he embraced friends he'd last seen half a decade ago, joked, remembered good old times, and said, "Mi casa es su casa."

Our guests brought gifts: bags of potato chips and gallon jugs of red wine. I told myself these offerings required my thanks, that my job, as hostess, had been to set the stage, not to control how actors used it; but I had relished my solitary preparations, and the arrival of guests felt like an invasion. H put Jimmy Cliff on the turntable, and the room became unbearably loud. I was the only one who knew no one; no one, that is, except H.

I was watching him. He was watching the front door. Each time it opened his eyes flicked toward it. *He's expecting someone, someone special.* An hour and a half into our event, she arrived.

She was everything I'm not: tall, skinny, with short-cropped thick blond hair that looked like she'd cut it herself, without a mirror, grabbing tufts and lopping them off in a fit of something. In spite of her unkemptness, or perhaps because of it, she was oddly beautiful; hers was an aesthetic of careless disregard—utterly different from my own anxiety-driven immaculate and orderly grooming. She had on blue jeans with a tear at the left knee and rips on the right thigh, a hand-knitted red sweater with a ring of reindeer at the level of her clavicles, and a macramé tote bag over one shoulder. A dog entered with her, a shaggy terrier mix. She went directly to my husband; they embraced. It was more than the embrace of friends, their bodies closer and the length of their contact more lingering. The room was quiet, everyone watching. It struck me that the people in that room had a shared past and knew things I didn't.

I stepped forward to greet the guest and her dog. I wanted a dog so badly it hurt. My husband said, "This is Melody." I shook her hand.

"What's your dog's name?" I asked.

"Dog," she said.

California 151

I extended the back of my hand to Dog's muzzle. My hand smelled of New Dawn and Barkeeper's Friend. Dog turned his head away. Melody smelled of patchouli: musky, heady, funky.

"Would Dog like a bowl of water?" I asked.

Though she answered me, her gaze remained on H. "We came in my VW bus. We've been living in it. It has everything we need. Dog's just had his water. But I'd love a glass of wine." She removed a small paper sack from her tote bag. "I've brought treats: acid caps. *Really* good stuff; there's plenty for everyone." She placed the sack on the table.

"Make that two glasses, Jo-Anne," said H.

The air felt viscous and my limbs leaden. In slow motion, or so it felt, as though I were struggling through thick matter, I moved to the table. My pumpkin candleholders had been shifted aside to accommodate the gallon jugs of red wine; my amber glass turkey had disappeared, replaced by a paper plate with a few crumbs of marijuana brownies someone had brought as an hors d'oeuvre; two of the gallon jugs were empty. I unscrewed the cap of a third, lifted the heavy thing, and poured glasses for H and Melody. They raised their glasses in silent salute, clinked rims, and drank deeply. A red drop landed below the ring of reindeer.

They turned to the door, Dog in tow, and were gone. I turned to the room. Jimmy Cliff was singing, "The Harder They Come . . ." Someone was air-drumming.

A guest called to me, "Hey Jane, we've got the munchies here. How's that turkey comin' along?"

I felt as though a thick pane of glass had come down between me and everyone else. I could see them, our guests—my husband's guests—talking and drinking, but I could no longer hear them. It was as though I were in a dream and knew I was dreaming and yet could not wake up. Like a somnambulist not in charge of her limbs, I lifted the heavy turkey off the counter where I'd earlier set it to rest in its artisan-made copper pan and carried it to the dining table; I placed carving tools beside it and brought out all the food I'd prepared from the recipes the staff at the Art History office had so kindly given me: corn bread, apple pie, green bean casserole, persimmon pudding, salad, pecan pie, stuffing, mashed potatoes, gravy. All of it I placed on the table without regard for proper placement for I'd lost the capacity for artful arrangement. And then I went into the kitchen and shut the door and pushed in the knob that locked it and leaned my back against it and sank down to the floor.

I saw that the floor was still dirty; the cupboard doors needed a good scrubbing; the oven had a residue of old grease. I had not done a good job; my cleaning was not up to Rosie's standards. I took out the kitchen mop and a bucket and other cleaning supplies and tried to channel Rosie and got to work and cleaned. And when I was done, I lay down on the floor and slept.

When I awakened, everyone had gone. They had partied; most of the food had been consumed; someone had thrown up on the living room floor and someone had thrown up in front of the commode. Perhaps that meant they hadn't enjoyed my repast, but I no longer cared. What I cared about was erasing their residue. As though I were ten Rosies, I cleaned.

I'd planned to make stock from the turkey carcass. One of my index cards from the Art History staff had a recipe titled, in caps: GREAT STOCK FROM CARCASS! But I couldn't bear to do anything with the carcass except throw it away. I opened a hefty garbage bag to tip it into, paused, then removed whatever tasty morsels still clung to bones and placed them on a clean plate. I did the same with the pies, stuffing, mashed potato, green bean casserole, and corn bread—a fine arrangement of scraps artfully arranged, for now I cared. Everything else, everything that wasn't on that plate of scraps, I tipped into the garbage bag, tied the ties, dumped it into the trash bin outside the back door, and fastened the lid with clamps.

A neighbor had warned me to secure the lid to our trash bin.

"Raccoons live in the back alleys," she'd said. "They're scavengers.

They come out at night and raid the bins. They're picky. If you're not careful, you'll find your refuse scattered all over your yard."

I'd been scrupulous in heeding her warning and always made sure the clamps were well-fastened.

When I was done cleaning I took the plate of scraps and went out into the silent November air of our barren backyard and laid the plate on the brick paving a few feet in front of the patio's only piece of furniture—a chair too worn for the previous renters to have bothered taking it away—and sat down on it, a mohair shawl draped over my shoulders.

For months, I'd been coming out to the back patio at night—always and only after H was asleep. I relished the dark silence and solitude and the cold clean air that hit me when I stepped outside. I'd sit in the chair and look up at the sky and try to accustom myself to the unfamiliar constellations of the northern firmament. It had been a shock the first time I'd looked up. The strangeness of the night sky made me feel I'd lost my way, and I wasn't sure how, or if, I'd ever find it again. Over the months, as I continued this practice, I became more familiar with the arrangement of the stars, and I came to understand that though the constellations above our house in Johannesburg had been familiar to me, I'd no more known my way there than I did here.

One night, several weeks before Thanksgiving, I heard a rustle at the base of the tall hedge. Turning to the sound, I saw a furry little face with a bandit's mask poking through the thick growth. Nose twitching, it looked at me, took my measure, then emerged on little paws beneath a short compact body with a long striated bushy tail. I knew at once it was a raccoon. Despite my neighbor's warning, I was surprised. The animal was, to me, so quintessentially American, so redolent with images of American frontiersmen that I half expected Davy Crockett or Daniel Boone in buckskin jacket and fur hat with a raccoon's tail to emerge through the hedge in pursuit.

We stared at each other for a moment, two creatures in an alien habitat; and then he turned and left the way he'd come; I somehow assumed the little animal was male.

At once I felt bereft. I'd wanted him to stay. I longed for him to return.

I sought to lure him back. I saved scraps, put them on a plate, and set it down on the brick paving when I came out to see the night sky. I'd wait as long as I could, but when the night air grew too cold, I'd take the scraps and go inside. One night I forgot to take the plate in. The following day when I remembered and went out to retrieve it, I saw the food had been eaten. In the ensuing weeks, I left out a plate of food every night. My offering was always consumed.

That Thanksgiving I resolved to wait up to witness my little friend devour his meal. The night was cold. I hugged my shawl closer, my mohair shawl woven from the wool of Angora goats, descendants of a small herd sent to South Africa in 1838 by the sultan of Turkey. The sultan, unwilling to share his country's lucrative mohair production, neutered his rams before he sent the herd; but the shipment's single doe was already pregnant. She gave birth on the ship to little billies and to the angora goat industry that soon flourished in South Africa's dry Karoo.

I hugged myself into its warmth. Perhaps I dozed. When I opened my eyes, there was the raccoon, examining the plate of scraps as carefully as a gourmet before a splendid spread. We looked at each other, and then, accepting my presence, he delicately reached for a piece of turkey; he sampled a piece of pumpkin pie, then one of apple; he sniffed the corn bread and took a nibble. And then, with gusto, dug in.

My Thanksgiving wasn't Rockwellian, but a little raccoon relished my food and my company. And I was grateful for his.

Empty Bookshelves

H came home the morning after Thanksgiving. He insisted nothing untoward had happened with Melody except dropping acid, having too much to drink, and passing out. We needed now, he said, to move forward and make things work. I wanted to believe him.

We started seeing a marriage therapist. I wasn't ready to leave the marriage. My baby was due in three months, and I hoped a child would get us on track. I was delusional. We bought a house in San Francisco with money my grandfather had left me and registered the house in both our names. To my first charge of delusional, now add idiocy—though in mitigation I'll add that I, an unemployed student, hadn't qualified for a line of credit. My inheritance from my grandfather was our down payment, but my husband's signature, his co-ownership, was necessary to complete the purchase. Contrary to my hopes, the house did not help. By the time my baby son was fourteen months old I'd reached my limit of what I could endure. I moved out and extended my maternity leave of absence from Stanford.

From our house, I took nothing except my son, his crib, his high chair, his clothing, my boxes of books (still unpacked), personal papers and journals, and my clothes. As I was loading the U-Haul, a neighbor brought out a bentwood rocker and set it on the sidewalk beside the truck.

"If you want it, it's yours," she said.

"It's a great chair," I said. "Why would you give it away?"

"It has bad vibes," she said. "I need it out of my house. Bad vibes for me, not you. If you're uncomfortable getting something for nothing, you can give me twenty bucks for it."

I gave her twenty bucks, and she helped me load it into the U-Haul. It had no associations with my marriage and the domestic interiors I'd shared with H. I was glad to have it.

My son and I moved into an apartment on Haight Street: small, with big windows and good light, on the third floor and no elevator.

I bought bookshelves on which I arranged my precious books (at last unpacked) by subject in orderly rows and placed the bentwood rocker in front of them. I liked how the room looked: bare and austere: the rigid geometry of a wall of books, the Art Deco arabesques of a single chair.

The apartment was close to Golden Gate Park; I pushed my son there in his stroller every day and sat with other mothers in the playground and watched him play; I made friends; I joined a women's childcare co-op; I met a woman from the Zen Center and learned to sit zazen; I enrolled in a massage course in which, naked, we massaged one another and, to loosen muscles and inhibitions, danced to New Age music. I found myself laughing and experiencing joy. I was shaking the dust of my marriage off my feet.

That whole time I never heard from H. I knew he was biding his time, sure I would beg him to take me back, sure I would call, sure I would regret my move.

My only regret was that I'd taken so long to leave.

When two months had elapsed, he called me. "I need to speak with you. When is a good time?"

I wanted to say *never*; I wanted to tell him I'd left because I couldn't bear to be around him and that I felt so much better without him. But we had practical issues to work out: finances and custody. I said, *OK. Today.*

He must have called from a nearby pay phone because almost immediately I'd put down the receiver, he knocked on the apartment door. I let him in and gestured to the bentwood rocker. I didn't know what to say, so I offered him a glass of water. He said he'd prefer a glass of wine, red, if I had it. I had a bottle in the kitchen. I uncorked it, filled a glass, handed it to him, and sat down on the floor, cross-legged, facing him.

He downed the contents and leaned back into the rocker.

"Please listen and don't interrupt," he said. "There's a lot at stake and you need to listen."

The monologue commenced—a litany of causes that had brought us to this crisis; a litany of reasons I should return to the marriage:

Your excessive emotionality, your difficulty in adjusting to a new country, your difficulty adjusting to motherhood, your tendency to retreat and shut down, your shyness, your reliance on your family, your difficulty making friends, your aloofness. I am a reasonable man. If you recant, I will take you back. We need to stay together because: (1) we share a history and (2) we have a bond not possible with anyone not from South Africa. We are—joking now—*both from the arsehole of the world, etc., etc.*

I'd half expected him to tell me he loved me, that he needed and missed me, that he treasured me for the qualities that are uniquely mine; half expected, half dreaded, and, if I'm to be honest, in some small part, hoped for—hoped, in my madness, to be the yo-yo I'd always been. But words of love were not in his monologue. I realized I was grateful, for I'd have had a hard time saying no to love—though for one tiny fraction of a second, I thought he was about to profess love, for he looked at me intently, seeming to *see* me through the swamp of words clogging the empty space between us. I held my breath, half longing, half dreading to hear what I did and did not want to hear.

He extended his glass. "It's empty," he said. "I'd like a refill."

He was slotting me into my old role of serving him. Under ordinary circumstances, I'd be glad to refill the glass of any visitor to my home, but these were not ordinary circumstances, and he was not any visitor.

I let his request hang in the air and slowly descend onto the pale carpet; I could almost see it. And then I arose from the carpet, stepped into the kitchen, stepped back with the wine bottle, and placed it on the floor beside him. He could pour his own wine. Taken aback, he fixed his gaze on me, commanding compliance. I returned his gaze and held it. He dropped his, lowered his head, bent forward at the waist, grabbed the bottle by the neck, and filled his glass, sloshing red wine onto the carpet. I did not stir. To hell with my security deposit. After a long silence, he continued with his monologue.

Internally I was shaking, surprised by my newfound ability to take a stand against him. I recalled the instruction I'd received at Zen Center and concentrated on my breath: in and out, slowly, counting sets of ten, my lungs expanding and contracting, the air ebbing and flowing in slow rhythm; a tidal flow of the life force that connects all beings; and I tuned him out.

I focused on the rows of books that covered the wall behind him; all the books I'd read and loved through my undergraduate and graduate years at the University of the Witwatersrand; books that were part of my history: *The Mirror and the Lamp*; *Romantic Theory and the Critical Imagination*; *The Great Tradition: George Eliot, Henry James, Joseph Conrad*; *The Well-Wrought Urn*; *The Liberal Imagination*; *Sincerity and Authenticity*; *Anatomy of Criticism*; *Mimesis*; *Culture and Anarchy*. My beloved books.

The clink of an empty glass against an empty bottle drew me back.

"You've heard me," he said. "I'll repeat. I'm willing to take you back. Don't rush. I'll give you a moment or two to think it over. You're basically intelligent, so I'm confident you'll agree that coming back is the most sensible, most rational course of action. I'm prepared to overlook this, this . . ." he waved his hand into the room, "this . . . and move on."

He closed his eyes and leaned back into the rocker, relaxing, pleased with himself.

"No," I said. "No. I don't need a moment. Or three, or four, or ten. My answer is no. No."

He opened his eyes, his face ashen, his body rigid.

"What? What did you say?"

"No. I said no."

I heard a sound from the next room. My son was stirring. I was afraid H would use the child as a reason to extend his visit and force his point, but he rose from the rocker and stood over me.

"You have made a mistake," he said. "You will regret it. I will make sure you will regret it."

I heard him go down the stairs. He was physically gone, but something of his presence remained. I felt it, a miasma spreading through the apartment, a miasma most intensely toxic in the space he had just vacated: the bentwood rocker. The effluvium clung to the rocker; it rose from the rocker to my bookshelves; it hovered over my books; wave-like, it spread into the room; it choked me. I could not push away the memory of the sight of him on the rocker against the wall of my books. That wall had framed him. It was inseparable from my image of him rocking back and forth, drinking wine, closing his eyes, waiting for my capitulation and his victory.

Was this where my scholarship had led me? To a wall of books framing a man I loathed, books from which I'd sought wisdom, books from which I'd sought guidelines for living? What good had they been? They were nauseating false props. I ran to the bathroom and threw up.

My son was crying.

I grabbed the rocker, lugged it down three flights of stairs, dumped it on the sidewalk with a sign scotch-taped to the back: *Free!* I raced up the stairs, changed my son's soggy diaper, made him scrambled eggs, and began to repack the books that I had, only days before, unpacked and lovingly wiped the dust from. I had to get rid of them, clear them out of my life. I still had the boxes. At last, they were reboxed. The day was gone. The sky was dark. The used bookshops on Shattuck Avenue, Berkeley, would be closed. No matter. I would leave them outside with a sign: *Free!*

Three trips later—back and forth across the Oakland-Bay Bridge, my son secured into his car seat, boxes piled onto the passenger seat, on the rear seat beside my son, in the trunk, on the floor—I was done. My apartment was empty. I carried my sleeping child from his car seat to his crib. It was time to exult in my purified and emptied space. To celebrate with a glass of wine.

I opened a bottle of white, poured a glass, and raised it to my lips. I'd expected exultation; I tasted grief. Kneeling before shelves empty save for a residue of old dust, I laid my cheek in the space that had held *The Canterbury Tales*, *The Faery Queen*, *The Pilgrim's Progress*, and *Paradise Lost*; I reached my left arm into the emptiness where *Time and Free Will*, *Matter and Memory*, and *Illuminations* had resided; my right arm into the absence of *Vision and Design*, *Saturn and Melancholy*, and *The Sense of Order*, and wept.

"You have made a mistake. You will regret it. I will make sure you will regret it."

What might he mean? What could he do?

I had not made a mistake. My only regret was that I hadn't left sooner.

I regretted the loss of my books. Regret in the old English sense: *to feel sorrow for; to weep or bewail*. For my books, I wept, I mourned. For them I longed to turn back the clock, to gather them in my arms, to caress their dust jackets, to inhale their musty odors. In the years that followed I would replace many. Though the titles would match those I'd thrown into boxes and driven across the Bay Bridge and abandoned in the covered entryway of a Shattuck Avenue used bookstore, I would never love the replacements as I'd loved those I never saw again. The replacements lacked my marginalia, the record of my dialogue with the author, my coffee, tea, and food stains, my wavy underscores, my dog-eared corners. My history.

What could H do to make me regret my *no*?

Consequences

H got what he wanted, but his "victory" confirmed the rightness of my decision to leave him.

His first try—his failed attempt—came a few weeks after his visit to my Haight Street apartment. By that point, through our attorneys, we'd established a visitation schedule: My son would be with his father every other weekend. I both longed for and dreaded the moment of his return: It was joy to have my child back, torture to have to interact, even for a moment, with his father when he handed over my child and a bag stuffed with the dirty laundry a child accumulates over a weekend.

When my son was gone, I felt lost, untethered, and almost unbearably lonely. To escape my empty apartment, I'd set off on foot across San Francisco. With no destination in mind, I'd wander—along Divisadero Street through the Richmond to Pacific Heights to the Marina to North Beach, up Telegraph Hill, through Chinatown to Nob Hill until, exhausted and footsore, I'd find my way back to my empty Haight Street apartment. Other times I'd head toward the Castro, the Mission District, and Noe Valley. The only part of town I avoided was the Sunset because H was there, in the house we co-owned.

On Sundays, I'd drive to Green Gulch Farm Zen Center in Marin County. In those days visitors could join the residential community to sit zazen, hear the dharma talk, and partake of a vegetarian lunch. I appreciated the quiet stillness and the company of strangers who asked nothing of me, not even a social exchange of pleasantries, for they all seemed focused on their breath, or on the careful mastication of vegetables and rice, or on keeping their movements economical and unobtrusive. Never at the best of times good at small talk, I was grateful at not having to produce it. After lunch I'd walk through the organic farmland to Muir Beach, sit on a rock, watch the waves, and try, like my luncheon companions, to focus on my breath.

One Saturday night, unable to bear another second in my empty apartment, I went to a bar. I wasn't there long before a man sat beside me and asked my name. I was awkward, unsure of the protocols of such an encounter, and more than a little afraid of the impulse that had led me there. Having given my name, uncertain whether I should have, I nervously sipped my cocktail, finishing far too rapidly a drink far too strong for my small frame. The man asked if I liked to dance. I said I adored dancing but hadn't done it in longer than I could remember because my husband, who I was divorcing, didn't like to dance. I felt suddenly and unaccustomedly reckless.

"There's a club next door," he said, "I'm a regular there. The DJ's great."

I paid for my drink, he took my hand; we left the bar and entered the club.

There was a crowd on the dance floor and strobe lights and neon lights and palm trees against the walls and streamers dangling from the ceiling; everything and everyone was moving and we did too and he had one hand on my waist and the other on my arm or shoulder or hand to spin me into and out of the bodies on the dance floor and I surrendered to a dizzying ecstasy of dance, the world falling away in a madness of wild spinning, joy, lightness of being, and exquisite happiness. It was, then, the tail end of the disco craze and I'd missed it entirely—would have missed it had it not been for that night.

He was a professional dance teacher, graceful, a skillful lead, and effortless in his movements. Though I've referred to him as a man, he seemed scarcely one, though he must have been over twenty-one to have been admitted to a bar and to have purchased alcohol. He was very young, boyish, with peach fuzz on his cheeks. I don't remember his name or his facial features. What I remember is the boyishness, the peach fuzz, and the dancing. And his body. Almost hairless, slight, young, and graceful. I remember it because, later, when he took his clothes off in my apartment and I saw his naked body—so slight and boyish, especially in contrast to the heavier, hirsute body I'd known in my marriage—I immediately thought of Edward Weston's photograph of his young son Neil. Weston's photograph floated in front of that man/boy's body, and I have never since been able to view Weston's iconic image without being taken back to that night. When I became a professor of art history and stood in front of a class of undergraduates teaching the history of photography, I would, upon projecting Weston's photograph onto my screen, feel myself back in the apartment on Haight Street, naked, with a naked nameless stranger I'd picked up at a bar. Perhaps the reason I cannot summon the stranger's face is because Weston, referencing and appropriating statues of classical male nudes reduced to headless torsos by time and vandalism, gives the viewer, in his beautiful photograph of young Neil, only a headless, slim-hipped torso.

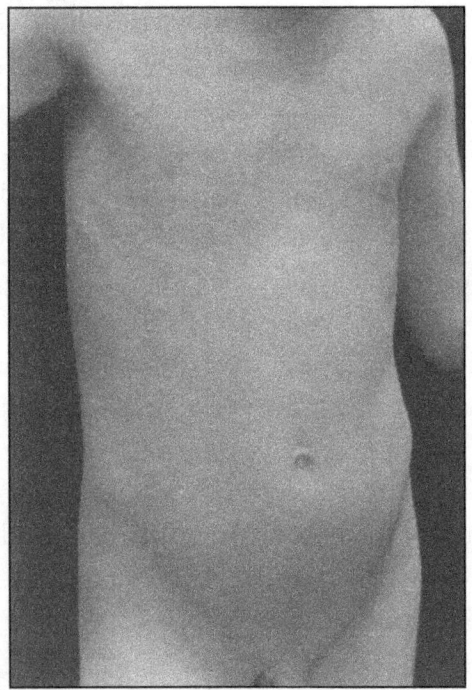

View of Neil, Edward Weston, 1925, Princeton University Museum of Art.

I never saw the nameless stranger again. A few days after our evening, I became sick: headache, tiredness, vaginal discharge. I sought treatment at the Haight Street Free Clinic. I had gonorrhea.

That was sixteen years before the passage of HIPAA, the Health

Care Insurance Portability and Accountability Act of 1995, and twenty-four before the passage of the HIPAA Privacy and Security Rules of 2003. The latter defined Protected Health Care Information as "any information held by a covered entity which concerns health status, the provision of healthcare, or payment for healthcare that can be linked to an individual." In 1978, my health care information was not protected; it was, in attorney-speak, "discoverable." And my husband, or his attorneys, discovered it.

I learned of their discovery during my deposition—a common part of the divorce process. I was in a conference room at the attorney's office—his or mine, I don't recall—with men in business suits around a polished table. I'd been answering questions for a while and was tired—as they meant me to be—for their final question:

"Have you ever had a sexually transmitted disease?"

"Yes."

"Have you ever had gonorrhea?"

"Yes."

"Did you contract it from your husband or someone else?"

"Someone else."

"Were you still married to your husband when you contracted it from someone else?"

"I'd left him and initiated divorce proceedings, but as you know, we're still not divorced."

"Please answer the question. Were you still married to your husband when you contracted gonorrhea from someone not your husband."

"Technically, yes."

They called me an "adulteress." Today, that label sounds quaint. In California, in 1979, the year of my deposition, it was, at the very least, anachronistic, for in 1969 California instituted no-fault divorce. This meant that misconduct in a marriage was irrelevant in the pursuit of the marriage's dissolution and that any property acquired during a marriage was to be equally divided. But my husband argued that our divorce should be governed by the laws of South Africa because we were married there. South Africa's governing legal code was Roman-Dutch, its principles based on the patriarchy of ancient Roman law, adapted and modified by the patriarchic Calvinism of sixteenth- and seventeenth-century Holland, which imposed its legal code on its Southern African Cape colony. This code was continued by the apartheid government. According to its law, proof of a wife's adultery nullified her claim to any marital property, even property she brought to the marriage. My husband and his attorneys argued that my "adultery" nullified my claims to the San Francisco house that I had bought with my inheritance.

Nice try, but we were official residents of the United States, subject to the laws of California. It didn't fly.

All along he'd held something in reserve, a second tactic should the first fail to achieve the goal he was after—at least according to what my father told me in a call from Israel: H's attorneys told my father that H had information that my father had illegally purchased dollars and illegally moved them from South Africa to a Swiss bank; that H claimed to have the name of the bank and the number of the account; that he would share this information with the South African Securities and Exchange Commission—an act that would result in my father's South African assets being seized and confiscated and my father, should he ever return to South Africa, being subject to prosecution. However, according to my father, H's attorneys were offering him a way out: H would refrain from divulging this information if Jo-Anne would sign over to him her share of the San Francisco house that he and she currently co-owned.

My father pressured me to sign. "There's more at stake than just your money," he said.

I remember the moment in court though it was more than forty years ago. The presiding judge looked up from our divorce papers and addressed me: "Young lady, do you realize you are signing away a substantial piece of property?"

"Yes, sir. I realize."

"Do you understand that you are entitled to one half of the marital property according to the laws of California?"

"Yes, sir. I understand."

"And you still wish to sign away property to which you are entitled?"

"Yes, sir. I wish to sign it away."

Why did I do it?

It was, at the time, a no-brainer. Though I'd been living in the States for almost three years, I was too caught up in my disastrous marriage, caring for my son, the culture shocks of an immigrant, and the challenges of a graduate program to form sustaining friendships. My only support network was my family—parents, sister, and brothers. They lived far away—in Israel, the United Kingdom, and South Africa. I was alone. Each night when I closed my eyes hoping for sleep, a picture arose in the darkness behind my lids: a giant screen filled with the map of the United States; just the outline; the outline as a frame; and within the frame, in the center, a small figure: me, cross-legged, my toddler son in my lap; just the two of us; alone in a vast empty foreign country.

Why did I sign?

I signed because my father told me that the stakes were high, higher than the value of my share of the house. The financial security of our family, he told me, was at stake, and he had labored too hard and taken too many risks to place it in jeopardy. It was up to me to safeguard my parent's future, up to me to make sure they could live comfortably someplace not South Africa, up to me to make sure that my siblings had resources to draw on should they need financial help—as I now did. If I refused to sign, the family would lose everything. If I signed, he would take care of me. It was just a house, and I should let it go. For the family. For the sake of everyone else.

I was to be a sacrifice. For the sake of the family.

In a way, he did take care of me. From Israel, he sent me money. My son and I did not go without food or shelter. For that I'm grateful. But I became my parents' dependent, and they never let me forget my dependency, my debt, their largesse. *We took care of you. You and the child. We supported you. We made sure you had everything you needed. We have been exemplary parents.*

But it wasn't true that I had everything I needed. Reduced to child-like dependence, I lost what little self-respect my divorce had given me. And I felt reduced in the eyes of my siblings, who resented me for the money I received from my parents.

What no one mentioned, what everyone—including me—forgot or repressed was that my father had given my ex-husband the information he'd used to effect his ultimatum and get my house. My father had been indiscreet, and I was the victim of his indiscretion. I didn't want to—couldn't bear to— think my father had betrayed me. I was too used to seeing him as my protector, my savior, as the wise paterfamilias. It was easy to accept my husband's betrayal: He'd been cruel and I'd come to expect the worst from him. Far harder—impossible—to accept and acknowledge my father's betrayal because all my life I'd loved and trusted him and believed he treasured me. He'd been the safe center from which I'd ventured into the world. That center, that safety, was now gone. Though I'd never felt I belonged in South Africa, I'd felt I belonged to and with my family. Now I was being told that my belonging depended on making a sacrifice. My belonging was conditional.

I spiraled into a depression that lasted, as far as I can recall through the murky memory of trauma, about eight years.

When I emerged from it sometime around 1985 and looked back, I began to think of those years as my nervous breakdown. I was, then, naïve about mental health and the language of psychiatric professionals. I now know that *nervous breakdown* is a layman's term, not a medical diagnosis. Because I'm now married to a psychiatrist, I know that *nervous breakdown* is not in the *Diagnostic and Statistical Manual of Mental Disorders*. Still, that's how I'm choosing to describe my condition: several years of a sustained nervous breakdown. And duration, I've learned from the DSM, is a significant factor in determining a diagnosis.

I don't recall acknowledging that I was undergoing a nervous breakdown. I did not seek therapy. Or, rather, I did not seek *conventional* therapy, the kind my psychiatrist husband practices. Living then in Berkeley, affected by its ethos, I turned to alternative approaches: rolfing, macrobiotics, veganism, acupuncture, meditation, tai chi—approaches beyond the compass of the world I knew. And, despite my nervous breakdown, I never stopped taking care of my son. He was my anchor, my grounding. He needed playdates, preschool, toddler gymnastics, doctor's appointments, meals, storybooks, regular hours. And so outwardly I was normal, responsible. A regular, attentive mother. No different from other single mothers struggling to recover from a terrible marriage and raise a healthy child while having, each week when I handed him to his father, to see the man who'd made my life hell and who, as far as he was able, continued to torment me.

I even returned to Stanford. We moved, my son and I, into married student quarters on the Stanford campus. I even completed enough coursework to graduate with an MA. But in a way, that was a failure. The program I'd initially enrolled in was for a PhD, but I wasn't up to finishing it. The MA was a consolation prize.

Though outwardly I seemed to be fine—fine enough not to cause worry to my family—I was not. One reason I know I wasn't is because I, who have a good memory, can scarcely remember anything from those years. That time is almost entirely lost to me, though it shouldn't have been, for night after night I filled composition books with the loneliness of my days, with accounts of my despair and attempts to assuage it. I wrote it all down.

I wrote it down because I needed to communicate—if only

with myself. I wrote it down because I wanted a record of what I was going through and was afraid I would forget. I wrote it down because I fantasized that I would reread my notebooks in a happier future when the pain of those days would be history.

But at some point, I don't recall when, I disfigured the notebooks. I have no memory of my act of disfiguring, no recall of whether I did it violently in a rage, or in a desperation of tears; if I ripped the pages out by hand and put them in a shredder or dumped them in the garbage with rotted vegetables and other muck. All I have to remind myself of my nightly outpourings are traces, eviscerated notebooks with broken words clinging to torn pages along the notebooks' spines.

Yes, I kept the notebooks, like I keep so much from my past. But when I opened them for the first time in many years because I *wanted* to look at the past, I found I'd gutted them.

Yes, I endured, but I've lost the record of what I endured, for I subjected those years to a double erasure:

(1) forgetting and

(2) destroying my archive.

All that remains are questions: what did I want/need to erase? What couldn't I bear to have a record of? Did I feel so silenced that writing my story felt futile? Did I rip out pages to act out my feeling that I'd lost my tongue and that to speak was useless? And why did I hang on to eviscerated notebooks? Why keep that reminder of erasure?

I have no answers.

And yet, and yet . . . memories from that damaged past linger, cling like bits of flesh to bone, like ripped pages to a notebook's spine.

I remember . . . going into a bookstore in the Castro and asking a stranger with gorgeous dark hair that swept across his forehead if he'd come away and make love with me. He said no and I fled in shame and embarrassment. I remember my shame, for shame lasts forever. I remember a boyfriend whose name was Tom who lived in a small apartment on Twin Peaks where he wrote bad poetry he wanted me to love, and though I tried to tell him what he wanted to hear, I couldn't bring myself to lie. I remember a man from Nebraska, a farmer, who asked me to marry him; his name was Bob and he was burly, destined to be stout, a Midwestern type, and I said no, though he was very kind and would have loved me forever, but farming life is not for me, though my son might have thrived. I remember a Thanksgiving with other single mothers, all of us seated on the floor in a circle around our children eating turkey and sweet potatoes off paper plates, grateful we'd escaped our husbands, though every one of us was lonely and longed for a loving partner. I remember making jam and researching how to taint a batch with botulism so I could leave jars on the steps of my ex-husband's house—my house until he stole it—until I realized he might put a spoonful on my son's bread and I would end up killing the person I loved most in the world. I remember a man from my hometown in South Africa, a masseuse for a major San Francisco sports team, who told me, after I told him about my fantasies of killing my ex-husband with jam, that he had contacts in the underworld who could kill my ex-husband so expertly that no one would ever trace the murder to me, but I said no, I can't do that because I have a moral compass, though my husband doesn't, and though I'm guilty of wanting him dead, I can't bring myself to be the agent of his just deserts, and, besides, he's the father of my son, and boys need fathers, however reprehensible. I remember a New Age therapist famous in Berkeley who told me to reach my arms out and call for my father, which I did, but then he asked me to show him how I masturbate; I remember my shock at yet another betrayal by someone I had foolishly trusted; and I remember thinking: I'm paying him to listen, but he wants to shut me up and make me a sex object; I remember having the good sense to get up and walk out of his office and never return; and I remember thinking I should report him to save other women, but what's the point when no one will listen, and, besides, I'm not strong enough to fight the system and file a complaint and go through all the drama that will surely follow.

Eventually, I emerged from my nervous breakdown.

I attribute my emergence to my move, in 1982, from the Bay Area to San Diego, where my parents had settled the year before. I moved because I wanted my son to have family. I moved to escape my ex-husband. I moved because I was lonely and needed family—even a family that had betrayed me. I moved because I got a job teaching art history.

And I attribute my emergence to time, which as everyone says, heals. With time, scars grow fainter, though they never go away.

And so began another chapter in my story.

7

Work, Love, Return

I WORKED AT A MUSEUM. I RETURNED TO GRADUATE SCHOOL AT UCLA for a PhD. I taught art history at UC Irvine. I worked at the Getty Research Institute. I taught art history in Canada. I was hired at San Diego State University. I made tenure. I published in top-tier journals. I made promotion to full professor. And I fell in love.

You met him earlier, in Utah, my husband Alan, reading a motorcycle magazine when I was reading Marlene van Niekerk's *Triomf*, but here's a fuller picture, though it's only a thumbnail sketch: He's the only child of an Italian Catholic father and a Jewish mother; a psychiatrist specializing in children and adolescents; a motorcycle rider and racer (Ducati, Moto Guzzi, Brutali, Aprilla); a collector of vintage British bikes (Triumph, BSA, Norton); and a snowboarder. He's funny and kind and somewhat obsessive-compulsive and sometimes annoyingly bossy, though he tempers it when he sees me bristle. His son's the same age as mine. We married in 1998.

I could end right here, thereby aligning my narrative arc with the Victorian novels that nurtured my girlish imagination: naïve young woman struggles to find her way in the world, makes mistakes, finds a good man to marry, and lives happily ever after. But I resist a tidy ending, for though I am a great-grandchild of Victorianism, grateful for its literary heritage and straitjacket moral codes, I am, more immediately, a daughter of postmodernism—inclined to metafiction and autofiction, to a narrative fragmented and choppy, to a surplus of self-questioning, to equivocation, to the inevitability of the unexpected, and to awareness that closure to a personal narrative, tied, however loosely, to my own life, will come only with death.

So this is a cesura, not The End.

After marriage comes the honeymoon.

I'd have been good with honeymooning in Italy, or Portugal, or Hawaii, or the Caribbean. But Alan, keen to see where I'm from, proposed South Africa. Anxious about opening a door to a past I wasn't sure I wanted to visit, I demurred. But I was curious about postapartheid South Africa and eager to please my husband, and so, in the end, I agreed.

My aunt, who still lived in Durban, was friends with the family who'd bought my parents' house on Innes Road, where we lived after Musgrave Road. Through her, we made plans to visit.

Alan drove us there. I was excited to see my old home. What I felt when we arrived was shock.

One of the pleasures of the house had been its openness: our fenceless garden sloped down to a narrow cul-de-sac and thence to a large public park so close it felt like an extension of our garden. Sometimes monkeys and peacocks, oblivious to boundary lines, wandered from the park onto the lawn beneath my bedroom window. I'd stand at the window and watch them: the peacocks strutting, the monkeys raiding the banana and pawpaw trees, though the servants, when they saw them, shouted *Hamba*/go away!

Now, thirty-three years later, approaching the house, I half expected to see peacocks in the garden welcoming me with their resplendence. Instead, what I saw was a ten-foot-high wall crowned with a rim of jagged broken glass and 220-volt barbed wire, the voltage proclaimed via a series of signs along the wall. A gate—it, too, electrified—barred passage up the driveway down whose long curve my siblings and I had run to the park, or walked to school, or to the corner shop for popsicles. A security sign on the gate read:

Warning! You are entering an unauthorized area. Property equipped with video surveillance system-intrusion detection. Anti-tamper, anti-movement, anti-cut. Continuous function surveillance. Optical fiber transmission. Focused mirror optics. Bullet-resistant door operators. Constant patrol.

No monkeys could now purloin bananas or pawpaws. No child glancing out the window of her bedroom would ever again catch her breath at a peacock strutting for a peahen.

I had read that crime in postapartheid South Africa was a problem, but I had not anticipated such extreme security measures. And I had not anticipated my numbed shock at the changes.

Alan parked our rental car in the narrow cul-de-sac. I buzzed the intercom beside the gate and gave our names. A woman's voice with a strong South African accent said, "Welcome! Please come in!"

I'd always resisted that accent, monitoring my speech to avoid the markers of South African pronunciation: the dropped /r/ in words like "water"; vowels forward in the mouth so that "penny" sounded like "pinny," "bad" like "bed," and "bed" like "bid." That avoidance was part of the ethos of Anglophile Natal, and my Anglophile mother sent my sister and me to an elocution tutor so we'd enunciate as though we weren't from where we were, so we'd sound more *British*. But in the short while I'd been back in the country, I'd found something comforting in that accent, heard myself involuntarily (and sometimes voluntarily) reverting to it, relinquishing my old habit of self-monitoring, abandoning myself to sound and inflection that announced: *Listen. Hear me. I'm from this place. I still belong.*

The gate opened, and we walked up the driveway. Jackie, the new owner (hardly *new* for she'd lived there for thirty years, far longer than my parents) was standing on the patio to greet us. Though I'd never before met her, she embraced me and inquired after my parents. She was older than I, but we shared a history, a landscape, an experience of place and time so profound that each felt she knew the other. I have had that feeling when meeting some, though not all, South Africans. It is at once comforting and deeply unsettling, that immediate connection to a total stranger whom one intuits as *family*.

"I'll show you the house," she said. "It was for many years a good home, though we've decided to sell. After the tour we can visit over tea and cookies so you can remember South African hospitality and I'll tell you why we're leaving."

She ushered us into the large living room.

Entering a house I'd once known intimately and that held a significant part of my family's history was uncanny—a disturbing compound of strange and familiar. I'd expected to see the house as it had been and remained in my memory, but everything had changed. Jackie's taste was different from my mother's—not the idiosyncratic, eclectic personal mix of antique and modern, but the tasteful, neutral product of a professional interior decorator so intent on harmonious balance that the effect—for me—was emptiness.

I felt unnerved, almost dizzy. It was as though I was being shown a stage whose set had been immutable in the chambers of my memory but that now, in the instant of a second it took to blink, seemed to vanish. Jackie's décor fell like a dark curtain over my memories.

To the unsettling unfamiliarity I'd felt from the street, I now added grief, loss, and even panic as the past seemed to slip away. And something else: a feeling that the lightness and brightness of the house—qualities I'd taken for granted—had been an illusion, a cover for something ominous that I hadn't, before, been aware of and wasn't, even now, able to identify.

And then I saw in every ceiling corner red lights blinking, surveillance monitors watching and recording our movements, relaying footage, I learned from Jackie, to some central headquarters. Heavily gridded accordion gates stretched across the French doors, screening the room from the sunny brightness of the garden. A room once open and airy had become a fortress and a prison, its inhabitants under constant surveillance.

I took a deep breath to cover my distress and took in the rest of the room.

The bar behind which my father had stood and revealed a secret for which I had paid dearly was still there. I walked across the room to touch its burnished surface and was startled to hear Jackie's voice.

"Are you all right?"

"Oh yes. The past overtook me. I should have anticipated that."

She led us out of the living room, past the kitchen, and into the dining room. The furniture was Scandinavian—blond, modern, expensive, with clean lines. I wondered if she expected me to comment on its elegance, but I said nothing, *couldn't* say anything. It struck me that the room *needed* blond furniture to offset the darkening effect of the heavy gridded burglar guards.

Compulsively polite and feeling the need to say something, I muttered, "I remember so many dinners in this room."

They flooded back: meals taken together as a family, all six of us around the table, my father at the head, my mother at his right; Marietta, our African maid, bringing our dinner on a large tray; my father, when we were done eating, calling in our cook to tell her that he'd sailed and traveled this world of ours, had dined and wined in great cities, but never had he eaten food as delicious as hers. She, embarrassed, flattered, and flustered, not understanding my father's flowery language, would first giggle then cover her face with her apron and rush back to the kitchen.

From the kitchen we followed Jackie to the formal living room which, in South African parlance, we'd called "the lounge" and to which my father, returning home from work, almost always retreated with a scotch on the rocks before shifting to his role as father and husband. I too had often sought the sanctuary of that room, especially when my brothers, who had the bedroom beside mine, had played and fought too exuberantly for my almost pathologic need for quiet. I had studied for exams there in a broad-seated chair in the lotus pose because I'd read somewhere that the interlocking of the lower limbs made more oxygen available to the brain. That room too was now under the surveillance of security cameras.

My biggest shock was the stairway and upstairs bedrooms.

A heavy accordion gate had been installed at the base of the staircase; sturdy crossbars filled in the gap above the bannisters; the landing at the top of the staircase was barricaded with gridded bars; every bedroom had a heavy metal door; the ceiling was studded with monitors and cameras; the view from my old bedroom window was no longer across the garden to the park but to the high white wall with electrified barbed wire surrounding the property.

"How do you live like this?" I asked Jackie, unable to contain myself any longer.

"We're used to it," she said. "You get to a point where you don't notice it—unless one of the monitors or panic buttons isn't working. *That's* when you notice. For a long time, this was enough, but that's changed. We need more security now. Crime's much worse. We're selling and moving to a security village at Umhlanga Rocks. Come, let's have tea. I'll tell you about it."

We returned to the living room.

"Gladys," Jackie called in the direction of the kitchen. "Please bring tea."

I looked at Alan, wondering what he thought of all this. He was from a blue-collar family. I was showing him a world light-years from his. I couldn't read his expression, but he reached for my hand in love and support.

An elderly African woman in a pale green uniform with a white pinafore, heavy shoes, and a *doek* covering her hair came out of the kitchen bearing a large silver tray with a silver teapot, a matching sugar bowl and creamer, porcelain teacups, and a platter of exquisite cookies. She placed the tray on the coffee table and curtsied.

"Welcome home," she said. "Miss Jackie, she tell me you live here long time. How you like the new South Africa?"

I wanted to tell her that being served tea by a uniformed African servant felt like the old South Africa and that what I most noticed about the new South Africa was the heavy security. But I said, "I'm happy to be here and to show my American husband where I'm from." Peering at the platter of cookies, I knew at once that Gladys had made them.

"Did you make these?" I asked. "They look like they came from a bakery in France; they're perfect."

"I make them." She giggled. "Miss Jackie, she say best in Durban."

"Gladdy's a treasure," said Jackie. "When she first came to me, I sent her to culinary school. I knew she had potential. My dinner parties are famous."

Still giggling, Gladys curtsied and retreated to the kitchen.

Jackie had her hand on the teapot.

"Do you still take it South African style, with milk," she asked, "or have you become American?"

"I've become American," I said, "but today I'll take it with milk for old time's sake."

She added a generous splash of milk to my cup. I grimaced, wishing I hadn't tried so hard to please.

"What's a security village?" I asked.

"It's the new thing," she said. "They're everywhere now. It's the only way to go. In this house, security is an add-on. In a security village, it's built into the design, with guardhouses and eye-in-the-sky cameras; it has private patrol cars and an office park, shops, restaurants, a golf course, and a school—all behind a secure perimeter wall. Our house in Umhlanga won't feel like a prison because the security's not visible once you're in. We'll be able to go for walks and not be afraid all the time."

She laughed. "It'll be like the old days."

As though with the force of an epiphany, I understood: Our house had felt light and bright and open because apartheid had supplied security for its white citizenry. Our open, fenceless, unalarmed property had been heavily guarded, as guarded and secure as any of the new security villages. I had not recognized or understood the extent to which apartheid had patrolled and surveilled our property and our lives, casting its panoptic gaze across the land, protecting the white minority from the vast, indigent, propertyless majority with its regime of passbooks, curfews, and programmatic dispossessions. We hadn't needed the intrusive presence of a fence, security gates, burglar guards, and red-eyed monitors because those measures were built into apartheid. Though our arcadian garden had been open to stray monkeys and peacocks, our bucolic paradise was built on repression, violence, and terror.

Universal franchise notwithstanding, the new South Africa was still the old South Africa. My father had been right to push us to leave, though wrong about the nature of the revolution: whites had not been massacred, but they lived in chronic fear they would be and sought, in the security villages of the new democracy, to recreate "the old days."

"Do you think about leaving?" Alan asked.

"Not really. We have problems here, but you have problems in America. There are problems everywhere. This is our country. I know Jo-Anne's father felt he didn't belong here, but we feel we do."

I felt a pang of envy. Since my father had told me that South Africa wasn't home, "belonging" had been my issue. I'd spent decades yearning to belong, uncertain what belonging meant, and wondering if I'd ever belong anywhere. But did Jackie belong? And if so, to what? To a gated community that kept the outside world out and where the people inside were inmates of fear? I felt grateful my father had never entertained that option for us.

We drank our tea, sampled Gladys's cookies, thanked Jackie for her hospitality, and left via the security gate.

I didn't know where I belonged, but it wasn't here.

8

Letters and Cards

An Archive

I'LL JUMP FROM MY HONEYMOON TO AN ARCHIVE, A PHYSICAL thing I've held on to for over sixty years. *Archive* may be an overly fancy word for a personal collection of letters and journals, but I like how the word's weightiness plays against my pretentious adoption of it—and against the girlish lightness of my record's original container: a pale pink box with an overlay pattern of white lace grown fat with cards and letters, the cover no longer closing over the unruly contents. At some point that I can't recall, I looped a blue ribbon around its width and length, then tied the ribbon into a bow, as though the whole were a gift. For me. For the future.

The box came to me when I was still a girl. It held a stack of pretty pink sheets with envelopes to match, a printed white lace pattern edging the corners. Notepaper.

Earnest, polite, and socially appropriate, I filled the sheets with thank-yous to givers of other gifts. I wrote my thanks in italics, the Italian fourteenth-century labor-intensive script my private girls-only school insisted was the only proper form of handwriting for young girls. Under the eagle eye of our writing teacher, we were taught to make *the downward pressure of the ink-charged square nib thicker than the angled fine upward stroke to effect an alternation of pressure and angle, a pattern of dark and light, thick and fine.* Our handwriting—like us girls—was to be visually pleasing, decorous, and restrained. Though I long ago rejected decorous penmanship, it's been more difficult to jettison the behavior traits careful penmanship was meant to instill.

I had a fondness for that box and held on to it long after I'd used and dispatched the sheets. What took their place were letters and cards addressed to me—including some I wrote to myself—aware, even then, in the careless bloom of youth, how evanescent memory is, how briefly its scent lingers. And so I made myself an archive, a place to hoard memory.

The dispatches I received span from the early 1970s to the late '80s. They came from family members and lovers in South Africa, Israel, England, and the United States. The notes to myself are mostly later, mostly from the United States, written from the pain and loneliness of a failed marriage and my long struggle to find a way forward.

At some point, the blue ribbon barely holding the contents in place, I buried the pink box in a larger one: a gray plastic legal file box, deep enough, I thought, for whatever cards and letters the future might throw at me. This container, this vessel for a vessel, hails from a different domain from the pink box. Its origin is the world of business, of men, and I chose it for its ubiquitous, neutral, nondistinctiveness. There was nothing about it to alert anyone who might seek to rifle through my things that the contents were private, charged, and secret, though I wonder now if the *anyone* I most wished to deter was myself. Was my primary reason for choosing a neutral repository to deaden *my* interest, a way to bleed color from letters that had seared my soul? I recall that I'd liked the gray file's utilitarian cover—on hinges with a clasp I could flick open with one hand and, with the other, drop in something I couldn't bring myself to discard, though decades would pass before I could bring myself to examine what I'd been unable to discard.

Time passed. *Drop in something* became *shove it in* as the contents of the legal file box, like the pink letter box within it, came to exceed its capacity.

No matter. Over the past twenty-five years, the time since my marriage to Alan, I lost the need to feed my archive. The cards Alan gave me went onto open shelving behind his chair in our dining room where I could see them framing his face during our evening meal. They always bore the same inscription, their message—that he loves me—ever constant, and so, while I updated the display as the next birthday or anniversary rolled around, I tended not to save his cards except in my heart. And thus, no longer in active use, the box, my archive, receded from the forefront of my consciousness.

I don't know what led me, one unremarkable day in 2002 when, standing on a stepstool in the little closet in my San Diego home office, searching on high for something I can't recall, my hand brushed against the nubby plastic and, as though in a dream, without conscious volition, I reached my fingers across its width, grasped, lifted, clutched it to my chest, and stepped down; whatever had sent me searching now yielding, like a dissolving image in a stereopticon, to the insistence of the legal file box and its adjacent pile of journals. I was, suddenly, aflame with desire to burst open the rusty clasp, dig into my hidden hoard, read my archive, and reengage with a past I'd tried to shove out of sight and out of reach.

I placed it all on my desk.

For years I taught a seminar at San Diego State University on memory, the archive, collecting, and museums. One of my favorite texts, one I assigned for several years because I loved it and because it captured the interest of my students, was a chapter from *Sacred Trash*, a book by Adina Hoffman and Peter Cole about "the lost and found world of the Cairo Genizah."

Genizah is a Hebrew word derived from an old Persian term for "hoard" or "hidden treasure," a concept fraught with the mysterious, for what was hidden away in *genizot* (plural) was textual material: religious manuscripts marred by errors in transcription; texts deemed dangerous or heretical; texts with Hebrew letters because the language, once reserved for religious study, was regarded as holy. Also buried were texts with the Hebrew letters that stand for the name of God—a name too holy and fraught to be pronounced and too sacred, even on a silent line of print, to be thrown away.

The Jewish communities who preserved these texts believed that, like the human beings who'd written them, they'd once been alive and were therefore forever sacred, not to be casually discarded but saved for future disposition in a ritual burial—part funeral, part riotous celebration.

The most famous genizah, the genizah of Hoffman and Cole's book, is the Cairo Genizah: a sepulchral, walk-in closet-size space in the loft of the ancient Ben Ezra Synagogue in Fustat (Old Cairo). The Fustat community, reluctant to throw out any text, gradually filled the loft with a vast range of dusty, fragile scraps of written matter that spanned the tenth to nineteenth centuries—sacred and secular, holy and not so holy, from manuscript leaves of the Jerusalem Talmud to butchers' bills, marriage contracts, and IOUs.

Starting in the mid-eighteenth century and gathering momentum in the late nineteenth, scholars, antiquities dealers, seekers after the arcane, and looters removed bits and pieces. A risky project. Risky not because access required climbing a ladder onto the roof and then descending through an aperture into the small dark loft; not because of broken rafters, shards of wood, stones and plaster from the collapsed roof; not even because of centuries of grime and dust that made breathing difficult; nor because of noxious insects that bit intruders, but because of two ancient beliefs:

(1) that a serpent—or serpents—lay coiled at the heart of its dusty chaos; and

(2) that those who dared glance at a sacred text would die within a year.

The legal file box on my desk made me anxious, and so I let it be, busying myself with class preparation and dealing with emails, though my eyes flickered from my computer screen toward it, and my hand wandered from the keyboard to touch it, to run my fingers over the metal clasp, wanting—and not wanting—to open it.

I told myself that I could not, at that point in the semester, afford the distraction, the disturbance of disturbing it. Truth be told, I was afraid. I began to refer to it as my genizah, joking to Alan that snakes had nested within it and would bite my hand if I reached inside.

Days grew into weeks. My genizah turned into an object whose presence I became accustomed to, even to the point of no longer seeing it.

At last, the semester over, my desk cleared of lecture notes and term papers, the legal file box again loomed. I closed the cover of my laptop, pushed it to the side, and pulled my genizah toward me. Flipping open the metal clasp, I reached within, pulled out the pink box, untied the ribbon, and removed the topmost letter.

January 23, 1980. From my father. From a new penthouse apartment in Ramat Hasharon, a suburb of Tel Aviv where my parents settled in 1979 after leaving South Africa.

To the west, a view of the Mediterranean.

To the east, a view of Gaza and Jordan.

From the land of his forefathers to his daughter in San Francisco, my father wrote:

Dear Jo,

I sensed in our conversation this morning and on the last occasion that we spoke that you were a bit off me. . . . You are entitled to your opinion, but I restate my view that you by having committed adultery and thus having invalidated the specific clauses of your ante nuptial contract and I by some still undefined act of stupidity made [H's] case impregnable and there was nothing we could have done except to have endangered the major asset.... All we gave up was some money which in the overall context is not too important.... I am for the moment happy that the lawyers are handling my application [for a green card] and hope to get a reply from them soon on the issue.

Had I read this letter before? Or had I, having begun it, felt so assaulted and violated and appalled by my father's words that I'd pushed it away, buried it for decades? I reread:

You committed adultery . . . invalidated the specific clauses . . . undefined act of stupidity . . . [H's] case impregnable . . . nothing we could have done . . . the major asset . . . gave up some money . . . not too important . . . happy that the lawyers, etc.

With prematurely arthritic fingers, my father had hit the typewriter keys. Poorly coordinated, a frustrated typist driven to this goddam machine because no one could read his impossibly illegible handwriting, his typing only marginally better than his writing, his fingers too short to stretch across the goddam keys, his fury at his frequent typos punctuated by carriage returns to the wrongly punched key, these errors overlaid by a corrective thrust at the right key or by whiteout, the sheet of paper was speckled, stippled, and dotted with blobs. As though he'd spat on it. Or hurled physical letters, letters as objects, letters as weapons, onto the white page. Were the larger, darker blobs a form of lapidation? Appropriate recourse for a father whose daughter had broken the seventh commandment, an infraction punishable by stoning the sinner to death, preferably outside the city walls lest her uncleanness infect the purity of those sheltered within?

The logos of patriarchy. The weight of words on a thin sheet of airmail paper sent across the Mediterranean, the Atlantic, and the continent of North America to the mailbox of a daughter's small apartment in a converted Victorian house on Haight Street, San Francisco, a city where she knew almost no one, a country where she was a stranger, seeking refuge from a terrible marriage that had produced a child, a small boy, whom she took when she fled her marriage.

I had forgotten the letter. No, not forgotten. Concealed. Repressed. Interred it in my genizah. Not because it was holy—though perhaps that twenty-nine-year-old *did* accord it sacred power because a father is to be honored, his text too, his accusations to be given weight. Or had she pushed it away because, all those years ago, she had sensed errors, a fragility in grammatical mood, an instability, that she, so fragile and unstable herself, had been unable to grasp, only sensing, but unable then to parse, feeling only at the moment of reading that there was something *wrong* that she lacked the strength to diagnose and pursue?

Rereading the letter in my home office almost forty years after I'd received it, I again felt its power, felt again an instinct to recoil, to shove it back into its place of concealment and forgottenness. Instead, I placed it under a river-rock paperweight (my own form of lapidation but gentler?) and took my dog, my beloved Max, for a walk, in sunshine, in the neighborhood I loved, the neighborhood that had become my home and refuge.

Walking, watching Max sniff and pee, his doggy engagement with the odors of sidewalk, grass, and tree trunk, myself warmed by the San Diego sun, something shifted. I reflected on the letter's mood. Not mood as emotion, but mood as *grammar*. We were, Max and I, *there*, experiencing our world in the *indicative* mood: he sniffing, peeing; I holding his leash, matching my stride to his; both of us feeling the warming sun, the comfort of our familiar route.

The grammatical mood of my father's letter was *subjunctive*—save for three words: *you committed adultery*. Indicative mood. On that foundation he built a house of cards: hypotheses, elisions, and conditionals—which allowed him to draw the conclusion he was after: *there was nothing we could have done except* . . . except what he, that young woman's father, elected to do: inform her that all she need do was *give up some money*—hers—because it was *not in the overall context too important* because not to give it up would *endanger . . . the major asset*—his money that he still, in 1980, held in South Africa and money he'd paid a courier to transfer to a Swiss bank according to the story he'd told her ex-husband so many years ago.

Not too important to her father was the house she'd purchased in San Francisco with money her grandfather had left her. Yes, she'd been foolish—stupid, naïve, the older woman judged the younger—to sink money into a house that she was obliged to register in both their names because his name—the name of the income-producing partner—was the only way to get a loan. Moreover, she was afraid of him, afraid that not including him on the title deed would drive another nail into the coffin of her marriage. And, besides, she'd held out hope that the house would be a nest, a safe haven where the marriage might heal.

She'd been wrong. The house had been a vehicle for betrayal, for a deal to be made by her husband and her father, a deal in which they'd sold her out and left her holding the baby—the only part of the deal that she embraced.

Because she had not, when she'd received her father's letter, been able to deal with it, she'd allowed her father's version—his explanation—of the loss of her house and the collapse of her marriage—to prevail, had allowed her family to understand her loss of independence and self-respect as her fault, and had then been made to feel grateful and beholden for her parents' financial support. Silenced by her father's allegations, she had become mute. Had *allowed* herself to become mute, tearing out the pages of her journals to silence herself.

What to do about it? The whole thing was, in a way, old history, and I had moved on. But was it old history? Had I moved on? I wasn't sure. My parents, my mother in particular, still reminded me often how much I owed my parents, how they had saved me. Perhaps the time had come to confront them, to rewrite the dysfunctional narrative they had lived by and continued to promulgate. Perhaps I should take the letter to their apartment, sit them down, read it to them, parse the grammatical mood and remind them of my father's indiscretion and its cost to me?

But even as I considered that option and fantasized doing it, I knew I would not. And I *despised* myself because I knew I would not. I rationalized that my father was an old man, frail, haunted by the past—as much by actions he regretted having taken as by those he had not. He slept poorly, his nights interrupted by terrors, by his sense of imminent death. He needed his illusions and the stories he told himself about the positive things he had wrought in the world—which were legion and for which I was glad to give him credit. He had, after all, loved me to the best of his abilities, and I, having much to be grateful for and loving him still, had neither the ability nor the desire to cause him pain.

But . . . what about my pain?

Again, I rationalized: Members of my family seldom apologize for or reconsider a past action that has caused hurt. Attempts to clear the air have, in my experience, generally made matters worse.

The voice in my head droned on and on, convincing me to do and say nothing. And so I resolved to let the serpent I had pulled out of my genizah return to his slumbers.

But he wouldn't! Though I wrestled with him, struggling to push him back into the box, he bit me and remained on my desk, coiled, ready to strike again.

I stared at my puncture wounds. I didn't want more. But how to continue with my father? Though I would not/could not confront him, the serpent had changed me. And my father, as sensitive to me as I to him, would know that something fundamental had changed. And though I, true to character, preferred to avoid confrontation, my father, also true to character, would seek it. The inevitable confrontation was triggered on Mother's Day.

Mother's Day

"I want to do something special for you on Mother's Day," I said to my mother two months before Mother's Day 2002. "There's a program of classic ballet highlights at the Civic Center. Shall I book matinee tickets for us?"

My mother said, "Perfect!" She loved ballet. It was darling of me to want to treat her. She'd look forward to it. A special Mother's Day with her daughter. She was a lucky mother.

I booked the tickets.

Eight a.m. Mother's Day, she called.

"Joey, darling, your brother Ralph just phoned to say he and Mary and the boys are driving down from Orange County to treat me to a Mother's Day lunch. I love to spend my special day with *all* my children who live in the States. Grandchildren too. It's so caring of them to want to be with me. You don't mind, do you, darling? I'm sure you can sell the ballet tickets and join us for lunch. Ralph's booked a table for 12:30 for all of us. It'll be lovely."

I minded. A lot. I was being dumped for the rarer pleasure of my youngest brother and his family. But, knowing that my mother had made up her mind and would be ungracious company if I insisted on the priority of my invitation and our plans, I swallowed my fury, though not the sour taste it left in my mouth, nor the sourness of my feelings toward her on a day I wanted to be loving.

"Alan and I will come to the restaurant to say hello," I said, "and then we'll leave. If Alan is free in the afternoon, he'll take your ticket."

The restaurant my brother had chosen was noisy and busy, as restaurants are on Mother's Day. My mother was bright and animated. I was the surly one. I placed my Mother's Day card on top of my brother's, and Alan and I left for the Civic Center.

Like many who struggle to express anger, my behavior toward my mother in the following weeks was passive-aggressive: I didn't call her or visit and, when she called me, responded with icy politeness.

About two months after she'd stood me up, I received an email from my father. An email from him was rare.

"Jo-Anne, your mother and I have something to discuss with you. Please be here Sunday at 11:00."

When any member of my family calls me "Jo-Anne" and not "Joey" or "Jo," I know trouble is afoot. I dreaded going. I couldn't see how not to.

When I arrived, letting myself in as I always did, they were seated on the white sofa—an unusual arrangement, for my father always sat in the wingback chair and my mother on the sofa—the two of them at right angles to each other. Now they sat pressed together, my father's left hip and thigh joined to my mother's right. Before them on the coffee table was a three-inch stack of cards toward which they kept glancing as though the stack were a fourth presence, an actor in a drama they had summoned me to.

In air thick with tension and expectation, I seated myself in the chair I always occupied, but I shifted it to face them. It occurred to me later that I, the accused, her fate decided before her trial, had voluntarily faced her firing squad.

Again, I had surrendered agency and allowed myself to be scripted by my parents.

"You need to listen and hear us out and not interrupt," my father began.

I wanted to say that I am the least prone in our family to interrupting, the most disposed to quiet listening. I said nothing. My father waited, his eyes fixed on me. I felt he *wanted* me to interrupt because that would give him a reason to fulminate.

"Your mother and I," he continued when I failed to fill the silence, "were distressed by your behavior on Mother's Day. You were disrespectful to your mother and your card was a disgrace." Leaning forward, he struggled to reach the stack of cards on the coffee table. My mother, eight years his junior and much more agile, grabbed the pile and handed it to him, but his arthritic fingers couldn't grasp it, and cards spilled onto the sofa and the floor. "Goddammit!" he spat. My mother, scrambling to gather the cards, laid them on his knee.

"Your mother and I," he said, "have been going through all the cards you wrote to her over the years. They're full of expressions of love—the sentiments a daughter *should* express to a mother."

His throat was tight. I could sense the explosive force beneath the tightness. I knew him well enough to know that he would not, could not, long contain it. He rifled through the stack, his recalcitrant fingers struggling to separate the cards, his agitation mounting as his fumbling failed to locate the card he sought, and the little stash again fluttered to the ground.

"Goddammit! Where is that goddam card!"

My mother, uncharacteristically docile, her lips pressed together as though to hold back the words that threatened to spill out, again retrieved them, found the card they had evidently planned to feature, and handed it to him.

"Read it, Sadie," he barked. She read. The card *was* full of expressions of love, for I had filled the white space surrounding the anodyne printed message with my own message, personal and tender. She paused to give my long-ago card and its sweet sentiments their due.

"Now read what she gave you this year," he ordered.

It was my mother's turn to fumble. I wanted to help her, for it pained me to see her awkward distress as, searching for the delinquent card, she pulled a card from between my father's slippers, another from between his knees, and another from under the coffee table. But to help her would have been to load the gun for the firing squad before which I'd been summoned, so I sat still, an observer and passive participant to the drama my parents were seeing fit to perform.

She found it.

"This, this," my father shouted, grabbing the card from my mother and waving it at me, "*this* is an abomination. This card has nothing personal. Absolutely nothing! Just your name. You owe your mother more than this! You owe her love and gratitude. You owe her words she can treasure! You owe her *everything*!"

That was my mother's cue. Her lips unpressed: "I no longer have a daughter in San Diego. You're dead to me."

I was used to her cutting tongue. I'd been its target more times than I could count. I also knew she'd later regret her sharpness, beg forgiveness, and "explain" that words had flown out of her mouth and she hadn't known where they'd come from and had not been able to stop them because they *just flew out*. I knew her so well I could write her script—which made her, at that moment, like an annoying fly, a distracting nuisance. I didn't want to focus on her. It was my father who had my attention, as he always did.

He paused to take a breath, and I, uncharacteristically and unwisely, filled his pause: "I was hurt when I wrote that card. Mom stood me up. She'd accepted my invitation and then, when something she preferred came along, backed out of our engagement."

I'm not sure he heard me. I don't think he was capable of hearing me. His face and nose were red with fury. Through snarling lips, he spat the words whose pressure had been building up in his chest and throat:

"Fucking academic, fucking academic. Veins as cold as ice. Fucking academic."

Again and again he spat those words. As though suffering from Tourette's, he repeated them. Again. And again. And again. He made *academic* an epithet, a term of abuse, of insult and derision. That thing that defined me, that I was proud of, my life's project, he made into an insult. He had taught me that the unexamined life is not worth living, that history and philosophy are worthy fields, and now he was letting me know that he despised my engagement with it all. I had followed his advice to make myself "exportable"; I had studied hard in South Africa, had gone to Stanford and UCLA and become a scholar, an academic, a tenured professor at an American institution of higher learning, and he valued none of it. I saw the spittle fly out of his mouth, saw the little droplets land on dust motes and shimmer in the light; I saw the little hairs in his flaring nostrils, and I involuntarily retreated into a state I had not entered in many years: dissociation. I became numb, a spectator at a ghastly scene that had nothing and everything to do with me.

Dissociated, watching him, I thought how accurate was ancient Hebrew to identify anger with the nose, for my father's anger seemed to originate in his nose, which seemed to "burn hot" as God's did when the Israelites transgressed and made a golden calf; and I grew fascinated by his nose, which seemed to lengthen as he inveighed. How wonderful is the poetry of the Bible, I thought, how inspired to associate anger with the nostrils. At last I understand the biblical passage! Next I registered the tartar on his broken yellowed teeth and wondered when he'd last seen a dentist and hoped he was aware that diseases arise in the gums and then enter the bloodstream, and how sad it is that elderly people often neglect their personal hygiene, especially their dental hygiene, and I should remind my mother to schedule an appointment for him as soon as possible so he could get his teeth cleaned. I watched his stubby forefinger stab and stab the air between us and wondered if he wished he were holding a knife and if he were, would he use it on me? And the more intense he became, the more benumbed I became. Correction: My limbs were frozen, but my mind scurried about like a rat in a cage, seeking a way out or, if I couldn't escape, a way to distract myself from the torrent of abuse my father was hurling at me.

It occurred to me, as though I were a critic who would have to write about this drama, that I would recount the details to my husband. To report accurately, I would need a precise tally of how many times this old man called his daughter *a fucking academic with veins as cold as ice*. I would not want to exaggerate or inflate the number. I would want to *report*. And so I began to count, though I had already let a handful of repetitions escape my tally. Ignoring what I'd missed, I began at one and went on from there: twenty-five, twenty-six, twenty-seven, twenty-eight, twenty-nine, thirty. Thirty was a lot, a substantial number. I could tell my husband *thirty* and know I had not exaggerated, and so I stopped counting, though my father did not stop inveighing.

After a while, rousing myself from my numbness, I said, "Dad, you should stop. You're going to give yourself a heart attack or a stroke, and if you do, I take no responsibility. You decided to behave this way, and you can decide to stop."

My interjection was like gasoline poured onto embers. My father, who'd begun to fade, regained his energy. I was afraid he would have a stroke, and so was my mother. Though her affront at my card had precipitated the confrontation, she, panicked at a situation out of control, sought to end it.

"What have I done!" she cried. "Morris, darling. Stop! Joey, stop him! He loves you. He doesn't mean what he says. Please, make shalom. Stop. Make him stop."

Her interruption reminded him of something else he wanted to say: "I've been thinking of writing you out of my will."

"It's your money and your will, Dad," I said. "You have a right to do whatever you want."

He paused, as though taking a moment to register my response. And then, his Tourette's tongue returning to the groove it was stuck on, continued his refrain.

Something in me snapped. I stopped feeling numb. I was weary, but I was also angry. It was a strange feeling, uncomfortable and unsettling. I felt as though the serpent I'd released from my genizah was now lodged within me, coiled and ready to strike. I'd been afraid of anger for so long, afraid that if I expressed it, I would not be loved. I realized now that my fearful repression hadn't helped. I was not loved. My mother had said that I was dead to her; my father had renounced me. I felt sick of them. But mostly I felt sick of myself for a lifetime of pussyfooting and placating.

I was, at long last, *angry*. Perhaps my father was right. Perhaps

I *did* have veins as cold as ice—not because I am a cold person but because I have always so assiduously tried to cool the heat of my anger lest it burn me up and singe the ones whose love I craved.

I rose. "I have had enough," I said. "You asked me to come here and listen to you and not interrupt. I did as you asked. And now *you'll* listen to *me*: You will never speak to me this way again. I will not tolerate it. Do not forget my words."

My father, his eyes closed, did not respond. My mother, sobbing between pleas for shalom, rose too and hurried after me as I went out to the elevator.

"Dad doesn't mean any of it," she said, pawing me and holding on to my shirt. "Please, please, Joey, don't hold it against Dad. He didn't mean it. He loves you. Oh my God! What have I done? Make shalom! I know you don't like to fight. You of all my children don't like to fight! Don't leave us like this. You're always so calm. You never get angry. Don't be angry now. Make shalom!" The elevator arrived. I wrenched her hand from my shirt, stepped inside, pressed the Down button, descended to the lobby, sat in my car, and gripped the steering wheel. I had to hold on to something. I heard screaming. I was screaming. And crying and pounding the steering wheel with my fists. It was terrible and exhilarating and exhausting and liberating. I had found my anger. It was a precious gift. I would never let it go.

My memory of the days that followed are blurry. My husband helped me through them. So did my therapist. My mother called me daily, begging me to forgive her, to forgive my father. I told her I needed time, and she should stop calling. I would call her when I was ready. She begged to know when that would be, and I could only repeat: When I'm ready.

At last, I was and drove to their apartment to resume my weekly visits. But I couldn't let what had happened go unremarked.

"Dad," I said, "we need to talk about what happened, about you calling me 'a fucking academic' at least thirty times. We have to talk to clear the air."

"I don't know what you're referring to," he said.

I didn't—couldn't—accept his denial.

"Here, in this room, after Mother's Day, about two months ago. You and Mom sat on the sofa with a stack of Mother's Day cards from the past. You called me a fucking academic with veins as cold as ice, and Mom said she no longer had a daughter in San Diego."

He closed his eyes. He didn't want me there, prodding and poking at his ancient being.

"I don't remember anything about it," he said. "I don't know what you're talking about."

"Well," I said, struggling to absorb his answer, "I suppose the advantage of being very old is that you can plead cognitive disfunction about something you don't want to remember."

Silence. He'd momentarily opened his eyes, but now he closed them again, pressing his lips together so firmly they almost disappeared. He wanted neither to see nor speak to me. And then he rose from the wingback chair, gathered his robe around him, fumbled with the tie, gave up, and said, "I'm tired, Joey. I need to take a nap. Please excuse me," and shuffled out.

And that, as far as he was concerned, was that. I never again brought it up. He wanted it papered over, and I went along with his wish, though the paper—at least for me—was as transparent and fragile as tissue paper, covering my wound with less effectiveness than a wet Band-Aid. I continued to visit my parents and to love them, but something had forever shifted. He knew it as well as I. I longed for the old emotional intimacy, for the sweetness of a daughter who adored her father, for a father who delighted in sharing his thoughts with his daughter. But that was over and had been for a long time, though I, not wanting it to be so, had been in denial. But now I realized it *had* to be over for me to move out from his long shadow and into my own light.

9

Leaving California, Finding Home

IN NOVEMBER 2019 MY HUSBAND AND I BECAME PART OF THE exodus of Californians to the Lone Star State. Our reasons for leaving included crime, taxes, congestion, regulation, and collapsing infrastructure. For years we'd visited Austin to attend MotoGP at Austin's Circuit of the Americas—the only US venue of the world's premier motorcycle racing championship. Like almost everyone who visits Austin, we fell in love with the city.

Leaving California wasn't easy. Except for one academic year teaching in Edmonton, Canada, I'd been in California since 1977—longer than in South Africa. It was home—until it wasn't. How would I adjust, how start again? My old question resurfaced: Where would I/could I/might I belong?

Alan found a house online that seemed suitable, and we made an offer. I flew to Austin for a live inspection and knew at once that it was perfect—on a greenbelt a short walk to Lake Austin in a tree-lined neighborhood a twenty-five-minute drive from downtown. We moved in two days before Thanksgiving.

It was difficult breaking the news to my parents. I was their only child in San Diego and felt responsible for caring for them in their old age. But my brother Ralph lived only ninety miles north. He, the youngest, the unexpected child of my father's middle age, was most like my father and his most cherished child, so it wasn't as though I were abandoning my parents to the care of strangers. Nonetheless, I felt guilty and promised I would frequently visit.

My first return was to celebrate my father's one hundredth birthday. For that milestone the family gathered: my father's four children and their spouses, his five grandchildren and their partners, and his seven great-grandchildren. From the United Kingdom, Pennsylvania, New York, Washington, and Texas, we flew to San Diego to join my parents and their guests in the elegant lobby of their retirement home. Each of his children and my mother made a speech. My father too. Visibly struggling, he hauled himself up from his wheelchair, a son on either side to lend support, and, in a voice gravelly but loud enough to fill the lobby, thanked us for coming, praised my mother, and delivered a storehouse of homilies accumulated over the course of his long life. We were his final audience. He who loved to give speeches knew it was his last. He spoke until he could speak no more, and we all cheered and downed what was left in our plastic champagne flutes, refilled them, and drank again—as much to celebrate as to quench the shadow of foreboding that lurks in the wings of a one hundredth birthday party.

Two weeks later we were back—a smaller cohort—to bury him.

He died from a fall, a blow to the head, a brain hemorrhage.

He took a week to die. I received a call from the hospital about his fall: "Your father fell and hit his head. He's in intensive care. Your mother also fell and is in hospital. Come at once."

I got on the next plane. My siblings, all three, were vacationing far from the countries they lived in; it took a while to reach and notify them. Upon my arrival, my mother was discharged but refused to leave the hospital, insisting on remaining at my father's side.

I'd long thought my father would not go gently into that good night, that he'd rage, rage against the dying of the light. But he slipped away, more peaceful in his dying hours than I'd ever seen him. Standing in his hospital room, an image of his brain tumor on the computer screen beside his bed, I photographed the scan. His brain looked like a moss agate, dendritic, with branching forms resembling leaves and, in the center, a dark swelling. I turned from the screen to my dying father—immobile and surrendered, tubing up his nostrils and in his veins—and photographed him. Beside him, only partially within the frame of my shot, is my mother, hands clasped, body slumped. I can't bear to dwell on either image. When, scrolling through the photos on my phone, I come upon them—my father's brain scan, my father slowly surrendering to cerebral hypoxia while my mother, desolate, keeps her lonely vigil—I hastily scroll past. And yet I do not, cannot, erase them. I keep death's presence on my phone.

In his last years, I'd wanted him to die. He was miserable, hating life yet fearing death, tough to be around. I'd felt death would be a release for him and everyone close to him—even for my mother, who did everything in her power to keep him alive, though he'd become verbally abusive, and she'd call me in tears almost daily and repeat the cruel things he'd said to her. I hated hearing them but listened. I suppose it was a bond of sorts, for she and I were the only family members on whom my father unleashed the rapier of his tongue.

Zikhrona livrakha. My father is dead. May his memory be a blessing.

Many years before my father's death, my husband—a long-term planner and more aware than I of the ephemerality of life, for he lost both his mother and his new bride before his twenty-fifth birthday—suggested we purchase burial plots. With a sales representative from El Camino Cemetery in San Diego, we traversed a green and lovely hill dotted with tombstones and chose our final resting place—a short distance from where my parents, some years before, had purchased plots. The day after my father's funeral I returned to his gravesite to lie atop his bones. And then I walked from his site's gash in the earth to the undisturbed grassy area where Alan and I will, when our times come, be buried. I lay on my back on the grass to rehearse my destiny.

A passage from the Hebrew Bible drifted down from the canopy of blue: "For dust you are and to dust you will return." I thought how far my family and I—and our ancestors—have traveled from the places of our births and about our restless wanderings in search of home. It felt peaceful to lie above my future grave knowing that we will all, one day, return to the ur-matter of our beginnings. Dust to dust.

Back in Austin after the funeral, I found myself lifting a prayer book from my bookshelf and turning to the *Mourner's Kaddish.*. For the next eleven months I kept it open on that page, and every morning, I, a secular Jew, postmodern and post-halachic, recited the ancient prayer. Involuntarily rocking like an old Chasid, I spoke ancient words whose meanings I did not know but whose significance compelled my daily observance. And each morning I was struck anew by the paradox of my practice, by my entry into a deep space I felt but could not comprehend, wondering what I sought from the spectral shadows that entered my room as I chanted: my father's shadow, the shadows of my grandparents and great-grandparents, and the shadows of the many unknown ancestors who came before, all with me and, at the same time, all receding into the infinite space of the past, all haunting my uncomprehending daily practice, my strange engagement with eternity and infinity.

Yit-ga-dal v'yit-ka-dash sh'mei
Ra-ba b'al-ma di-v'ra chir-u-tei
May his memory be a blessing.

During this mourning period, longing for more than my own solitary engagement with ancient prayer, craving community, I explored Jewish congregations in Austin and found what I was seeking, what I had, I realized, been seeking for a long time—a congregation led by an inspiring rabbi deeply knowledgeable about Jewish texts. Alan and I became members. The community welcomed us. Now, weekly, I attend Torah study, digging with fellow congregants into the mysteries of the tradition I was born into. And to better understand the language of the Torah and the prayer book, I'm studying biblical Hebrew.

A little over a year ago, when I was still working on this manuscript, still struggling to answer my two most pressing questions—Who am I? and Where do I belong?—Hamas terrorists invaded Israel's sovereign space and attacked, mutilated, raped, killed, and kidnapped Israeli citizens attending a peaceful concert and taking care of their families in their homes. Though I was already engaged with my Jewish heritage, the horrors of October 7 intensified that engagement. The pain of that day and the Judeophobia that reared its hideous head in its aftermath brought home to me that I am, before any other identity that might attach to me, Jewish. As Rabbi Jonathon Sacks writes so beautifully in *A Letter in the Scroll*, I know myself to be definitively "part of a people, involved in its fate, implicated in its destiny, caught up in its tragedy, exhilarated by its survival."

I am a Jew. That is where I belong.

Epilogue

I might have ended here, but still I cannot let go, cannot (yet) walk away. It surprises me, this compulsion to keep going, to take up more space; surprises me because all my life I've held back from taking up space and have been more apt to keep my own counsel than to share my thoughts. But even with almost 66,000 words behind me, I haven't yet captured what I set out to write.

Perhaps the issue is not so much "writing" as *imaging*. It occurs to me that I might more fully express the journey of this autofictional protagonist via an *allegory*, a visual image that succinctly contains and conveys her sense of journey and self. After all, I'm an art historian, and visual images are as much part of my vocabulary as words.

For a definition of allegory, I turn to Craig Owens's two-part essay: "The Allegorical Impulse: Toward a Theory of Postmodernism."

"... Allegory occurs whenever one text is doubled by another.... In allegorical structure ... one text is read *through* another."

What image might "double" my text and serve as an allegory?

Finding the image was not difficult. I didn't need to look. The image found me, floating into consciousness and becoming ever more insistent: Eva Hesse's *Hang-up*. And so I pulled it up on my computer screen and stared at it, wondering what my unconscious was telling me.

Here it is:

Eva Hesse, *Hang Up*, 1966, Acrylic on cloth over wood, acrylic on cloth over steel tube, The Art Institute of Chicago

The layperson sees a cloth-wrapped/bandaged square frame; a length of steel tubing emerging from the upper left edge. The tubing dangles down into the space in front of the frame, then reinserts into the lower right edge. There is nothing within the frame but the blank wall.

The student/teacher of Late Modernism sees more: The frame's rectangularity references the masculinist ethos of Minimalism. But Minimalism's hard-edged authoritative clarity is undercut by the bandage—a softening, emotion-fraught, feminist/female intervention.

Here is how the sculpture speaks allegorically to this art historian/writer/seeker of home: This is an injured frame, a frame that has been hurt and bears scars. Though hurt, it has endured. The steel tubing is an umbilicus searching in space for a place to attach to. Forlorn, not finding a place out there, it returns to the frame whence its journey began and connects.

In 2003 I saw Eva Hesse's retrospective at San Francisco's MOMA.

I walked through that show in tears, an experience and encounter with art I'd never had before and haven't since. I didn't, at the time, understand why the show affected me so much. Years later, I'm closer to that understanding. And grateful to Eva Hesse.

What I attempted to do in these many pages is consider the frame I was born into, to inquire how and in what ways I was framed, how and in what ways I've struggled against those frames—both the frames imposed on me and the frames I tried to fit into. In the end—and now I *have* reached The End—I find myself tethered by an umbilicus I cannot sever and don't want to sever so that, though I may, at times, have reached as far as it would allow me, I am always drawn back to and tethered to the frame that made me. And I'm grateful for that frame. It's home. It's where I belong.

Acknowledgments for Licensing Permissions

I am grateful to the following institutions for permissions to reproduce the images in this book:

African Pictures Library/African Media Online, for Laurie Bloomfield's photograph, *Cato Manor*, 1960.

The Gemaldegalerie, Berlin, for Vermeer's *The Glass of Wine*, 1660.

The Rijksmuseum, Amsterdam, for *Portrait of a Man, probably Bartholomeus Vermuyden*, (1616/17—1650) by Dirck Craey.

The Rijksmuseum, Amsterdam, for *Portrait of Jan van Riebeeck (1619—77) Commander of the Cape of Good Hope and of Malacca and Secretary of the High Government of Batavia*, anon, 1660.

The Metropolitan Museum of Art, New York, for Thomas Cole's *View from Mount Holyoke After a Thunderstorm, Northampton, Massachusetts*, 1836.

The Princeton University Museum of Art for Edward Weston's *View of Neil*, 1925.

The Chicago Institute of Art for Eva Hesse's *Hang Up*, 1966.

I owe thanks to Diana Edkins of Art Resource for her help and patience in obtaining copyright permissions.

The poem "Dreaming of Home," by Merle Feld, is from *finding words* by Merle Feld, URJ Press, New York, NY 2010. My thanks to the author for granting permission to include a poem so meaningful to me.

The photograph of my father and his factory is from *Durban 1824—1974*. The book was produced by the Mayor's Parlour, 1974. It was not possible to track a publisher or any persons connected to its production.

Family photographs are from family albums.

About the Author

Jo-Anne Berelowitz is an art historian, essayist, adventurous cook, sourdough baker, exercise and health nut, a dog lover, wife, mother, grandmother, an avid reader, and student of the rich heritage of Judaism. Born in South Africa, she emigrated to the United States in 1977 and lived in California for forty years. In 2019, Jo-Anne, her husband, and their Soft-Coated Wheaten Terrier, Max, moved to Austin, Texas, to live atop a greenbelt that harbors rattlesnakes, copperheads, scorpions, and many beautiful birds.

www.ingramcontent.com/pod-product-compliance
Lightning Source LLC
LaVergne TN
LVHW091539030426
835323LV00043BA/712